To: PAT

MW00593703

DANDY

A Jewish Boxer's Journey
From Russian Immigrant to Boxing Champion

Daniel Patrick Joseph

Dandy–A Jewish Boxer's Journey from Russian Immigrant to
Boxing Champion

978-0-615-52358-3

Copyright © 2011 Daniel P. Joseph all rights reserved. No part of
this publication may be reproduced, stored in a retrieval system, or
transmitted in any form or by any means (electronic, mechanical,
photocopying, recording, or otherwise) without either the prior
written permission of the publisher or a license permitting
restricted copying in the United States or abroad.

The scanning, uploading, and distribution of this book via the
Internet or via any other means without the permission of the
publisher is illegal and punishable by law. Please purchase only
authorized electronic editions, and do not participate in or
encourage piracy of copyrighted materials.

Printed in the United States of America

For Dad

DANDY

**A Jewish Boxer's Journey
From Russian Immigrant to Boxing Champion**

Moishe Josofsky at age 8 in Grigoriopol, Russia

PROLOGUE

There was a time when the sport of boxing was dominated by Jewish boxers. Yet even if you are an ardent boxing fan it's not likely that you would be able to name many Jewish boxers beyond, perhaps, Benny Leonard, Barney Ross, Ruby Goldstein, and Maxie Rosenbloom. But in the 1920s and 1930s, the sport was an attractive outlet for Jewish immigrants and second generation American Jews who realized they could make a living being a prizefighter without the fear of anti-Semitism. Not only did Jews discover that this sport was dependent on their abilities as fighters, but they also became managers, promoters, and trainers.

During the 1920s, nearly one-third of all professional boxers were Jewish. While Jews were winning thirty world championships between 1910 and 1940, there were many more boxers who were winning various other levels of championships. Boxers like Kewpie Calendar, Frankie Gilman, Benny Vogel, Bud Ridley, Cyclone Yelsky, Jack Josephs, Sammy Gordon, and countless others toiled in the ring trying to win one of those championships. But unlike those mentioned, one such Jewish immigrant boxer did attain a championship belt. Many Jewish immigrants struggled after first arriving from Europe, including pre-Soviet Russia, after the turn of the 20th century and many responded to the allure of the boxing ring. This is the story of a Jewish immigrant who was able to attain success in the ring and become a champion. This is the story of Dandy Dillon.

In the clearing stands a boxer
And a fighter by his trade
And he carries the reminders
Of ev'ry glove that layed him down

Paul Simon "The Boxer"

Anti-Jewish Pogroms in Odessa, Russia in the early 1900's

GRIGORIOPOL, RUSSIA

Percy Buzza, the Canadian Flyweight Champion, lay sprawled on the canvas of the boxing ring at the Board of Trade Building in Winnipeg, Manitoba, Canada, victim of a crushing right hand to the heart by Dandy Dillon. The match had been controlled by Dillon from the outset and when he landed his vicious blow to Buzza's chest after fifty-six seconds of the ninth round, the seventeen-year-old Russian Jewish immigrant became the undefeated Flyweight Champion of Canada in only his thirteenth bout as a professional boxer. On December 8, 1920, after thirteen fights, including four knockouts and a record of nine wins and four draws, Moishe Josofsky achieved something he never imagined growing up in Czarist Russia, a boxing championship.

Moishe Josofsky was born on July 14, 1903, in the small Russian village of Grigoriopol. Located eighty-two miles North West of Odessa and the Black Sea, Grigoriopol was comprised of Jewish peasants engaged in farming, handicrafts, and trading. Moishe's father earned a modest living working in a garment factory while Moishe and his six brothers and sisters helped their mother in their small farmhouse. Moishe was the youngest of the seven siblings-four boys and three girls.

Life in Grigoriopol was not pleasant. When the town wasn't being harassed by the Czarist troops riding through the town on horseback, residents found themselves trying to escape the ravages of the "pogroms." Pogroms, the term given to the large-scale wave of anti-Jewish riots that swept through Imperial Russia in 1881-1884, were believed to have begun as early as 1821 in Odessa. Other sources indicate that the first pogrom was the 1859 riots in Odessa.

The riots of 1881-1884 were triggered by the assassination of Czar Alexander II, for which many blamed the Jews. However, the local economic conditions contributed greatly to the rioting because of the perception that the Jews created competition. One of the close associates of the assassins of the Czar was indeed Jewish, but the fact was that the other assassins were all Christians. However, this had little impact on the anti-Semitic sentiment.

It was the much bloodier wave of pogroms that broke out in 1903-1906, which was estimated to have left more than 2,000 Jews dead and many more wounded, that caused the Jews to take up arms to defend their families. No one was spared during the riots, as women and children were often victims of the reign of terror.

In April 1903, riots broke out after a Christian child was found murdered. Although it was clear that the boy had been killed by a relative, the government chose to call it a ritual murder plot by the Jews. The mobs were incited by the anti-Semitic newspaper "Bessarabetz." During three days of rioting, forty-seven Jews were killed, over five hundred wounded, and over seven hundred houses destroyed. This pogrom was instrumental in convincing tens of thousands of Russian Jews to leave to go to the West.

Over time, the violence and anti-Semitic sentiment caused Moishe's father to seek a new and better life for his family. No longer could the family live in terror, wondering if they would escape the next wave of violence. He wanted to protect his family and shield them from the violence, hatred, and anti-Jewish sentiment that seemed to be deep rooted in his village. They lived in constant fear of being beaten, robbed, or even killed by their neighbors. He wanted to bring his family to America.

Beyond the violence, life was simple in Grigoriopol, but hard. Moishe would spend his days helping around the small farmhouse and playing with his older brothers while his sisters helped their mother with household chores and cooking. The winters could be brutally cold and the small house seldom kept everyone warm. The family, however, was very close knit so they endured the hardships happily.

Nathan and Eva Josofsky were proud parents. The children never got into trouble and they all contributed to the upkeep of the house. Nathan worked hard. His days were long in the garment factory nonetheless he always made time for the children. But now, he wanted much more. He wanted to make a better life for his family and to secure their safety.

In 1910, unclear as to where and how he would accomplish this endeavor, Moishe's father made the decision that he and his oldest son, Samuel, would to go to America to seek out a new place where they could move and help clear the path for the rest of the family. It would be tough on the rest of the family and at seven years old, Moishe would miss his father dearly.

Samuel was nineteen years old when he and Nathan began their mission. The journey was not easy. It took months for them to get to their destination working their way through Eastern Europe. But, eventually they made their way to Bremen, Germany, and found passage on a steamship.

The steamship they sailed in was not very large and hundreds of people were crowded into them. Most immigrants, like themselves, were poor and travelled in the lowest or steerage class. Nathan and Samuel found the living conditions horrible and watched many of their fellow passengers come down with various forms of disease.

After the long journey, they landed at Ellis Island in New York. Here the surname of Josofsky became shortened to Joseph. They worked their way west until they eventually found their way to Minnesota where many Jews before them had settled down.

In the first part of the 19th century Jewish immigrants from Central Europe came to America and settled in the larger cities like New York, Philadelphia, and Baltimore. However, a growing number of Jews made their way to smaller cities like Cincinnati, Cleveland, St. Louis, and Minneapolis. Between 1881 and 1924 over two- and one-half million Eastern European Jews came to America from their native lands due to economic conditions and religious persecution. The Josofsky family was among them.

Nathan and Samuel found jobs quickly and began saving every penny they earned. Meanwhile, back in Grigoriopol, the rest of the family had a heavier burden to take on without them there. Sixteen-year old David, the oldest boy left behind, had to assume a greater role in taking care of the family. He watched over Moishe, his brother Yankel, and sisters Sarah, Yenta, and Eida. It was during this time that Moishe became very close to his brother Yankel who was only three years older than him. They played and wrestled with each other constantly.

Eva was a strong woman who was not afraid of the challenge before her. She made do primarily with the foodstuffs generated by the small garden in the rear of the farmhouse. David took on odd jobs to supplement the finances that Nathan and Samuel had left for them and the three sisters occasionally took on laundry and sewing jobs. The family survived adequately, but not without some hardship. However, most of all, they missed Nathan and Samuel.

Finally, in early 1911, Eva received what she had been longing for, a letter from Nathan, saying that they had arrived in America and had found housing. They had found their way, along with other Jewish families, to Minneapolis. Nathan found work in a tobacco factory while David found a job in a meat market.

After learning that a home would be waiting for them in the new world, the family began preparation for their journey. They sold what little furniture they had to others in the village. Before he left, Nathan had sold the farmhouse to another family in the village so that they would have money for their journey and to provide enough money for the family to survive on until they were reunited. The purchasers had agreed to let them stay in the farmhouse, as part of the negotiated price, until they heard back from Nathan.

The family prepared for their journey with the assistance of their friends in the village. David huddled the family together and told them of the new life they would be going to in America. So, in the spring of 1911, following the same path set forth by Nathan and Samuel earlier, the family set out on their journey, a journey that would eventually land them in Minneapolis to be reunited with Moishe's father and brother. A new life had begun.

Immigrants arriving in America circa 1900

AMERICA

It was a long and arduous journey for eight-year-old Moishe. But it was a journey that Moishe welcomed. No longer would he have to be awakened by the sounds of Czarist soldiers marching through the streets of town, terrorizing all they encountered. No longer would he have to hear the screams of women and children, and the anguished cries of his neighbors fending off beatings by people shouting anti-Jewish sentiments. He didn't know what America had in store for him, but he knew that he wanted to be there.

Upon entering the United States, the Josofsky family name changed. A year earlier when Nathan and Samuel arrived, expediency dictated that the name become more American if they were to assimilate into the new culture so, it was shortened simply to "Joseph." There was also a new language to learn. Back home Moishe spoke primarily Yiddish. He knew some Russian, but when speaking with family and members of the community only their native Jewish tongue was primarily used.

In the months that Nathan and Samuel worked in Minneapolis, prior the arrival of the rest of the family, they were able to save enough money to rent a house large enough for the family to live in. Before this, Nathan and Samuel boarded in rooming houses. When the rest of the family arrived in the summer of 1911, they were able to move into a modest three-bedroom house. The three sisters shared one room while the four brothers shared another.

Immediately, life was better for the family. Albeit, there were adjustments to be made, not the least of which was adjusting to the family's new names. Yankel took on the name of Jack while Moishe became Danny. He retained a variation of his name Moishe as his middle name, Morris. He was now Daniel Morris Joseph.

Jack and Danny soon began school in the new country and adapted well. They learned English quickly because they needed to keep up in school. At the age of eleven and eight years old, they picked up the local language, but not without some obstacles. While they were often ridiculed by others in school because of the difficulty they had at first, they found comfort in the fact that many of their classmates were Jewish immigrants themselves.

Within a few years, Jack and Danny found that they had their bedroom to themselves. Samuel's job in the meat market grew while David became gainfully employed in a haberdashery. They both met their wives, married, and started families of their own.

When Danny was eleven years old, he got his first job. Jack had gotten a job selling newspapers about a year earlier and encouraged his little brother to do the same. So Danny went to work with Jack one day and was able to land a similar job selling newspapers on the corners in downtown Minneapolis.

While selling newspapers wasn't a particularly strenuous job, it was not without its hazards. Selling newspapers was a territorial venture. Those that had "control" of the corners at the busiest intersections usually made the most money. However, control of those intersections required tenacity and in many cases, strength.

While growing up in Minneapolis, Danny experienced his share of bullies in school. Danny was small in stature and avoided the bullies at all costs. He'd had his share of being pushed around and taken advantage of, but Danny never had been involved in a real fight. That would soon change.

After getting his new job, Danny settled in on a local corner near downtown Minneapolis. Jack had told Danny what to expect in his new job, but Danny was soon to learn first-hand what his new job entailed. In 1914, the traffic was comprised of a combination of automobiles and horse-drawn buggies. Traffic was light at Danny's first corner. While he sold the occasional newspaper to the infrequent pedestrians, vehicular traffic was light, consequently Danny would end his day with very little to show for his efforts. When he returned to the newspaper warehouse in the evenings to turn in his money and collect his wages, he was usually admonished by his boss for not selling many newspapers.

One day, Danny decided to move to a new corner where the traffic was much heavier in an effort to increase his earnings. He moved closer to the heart of the downtown area. Sure enough, Danny began selling newspapers in swift fashion. After standing on his new corner for the day, Danny tripled his earnings. This went on for several days earning the respect of his boss. However, some of the other boys soon learned of little Danny's new found success and became jealous. Somehow, Danny had stumbled onto a corner that was usually reserved for boys employed much longer than he.

Control of a profitable corner usually required several things: luck, opportunity, and strength. Competition was tough, and the older and stronger boys would take over the corners that they viewed as more successful from the smaller boys. Danny was to find this out soon enough.

Early one afternoon as Danny was hawking his wares on his corner, he was approached by an older, larger boy. Danny was told in no uncertain terms to leave the corner and find new ground. Danny, though, was stubborn and unwilling to simply leave as commanded. When Danny refused to leave, the other boy became physical. He started shoving Danny ordering him to leave. Danny firmly stood his ground. The shoving soon escalated into slugging as the bigger boy punched Danny in the arm.

Danny remained steadfast. The larger boy, undeterred, soon punched Danny in the stomach causing him to drop his newspapers and slump over in order to catch his breath. After a few seconds, Danny regained his breath. However, Danny's temper had finally taken hold and he lunged at the larger boy unloading a barrage of punches that landed time and time again on the boy hitting him in the stomach, arms, and face. Surprised more than anything, the larger boy struck back, but Danny was able to fend off the boy's attack and counter with his own series of punches. Unfortunately for the larger boy, Danny's punches kept hitting the mark. Soon the boy stopped his attack and retreated. Danny stood up looking at the boy with his fists clenched, eyes glaring and told him, "This is my corner." The larger boy, humiliated, said nothing, turned, and walked away. And with that, Danny had experienced his first fight.

Danny's experience that day was to be repeated from time to time as he was called upon to defend his territory. However, over time, the challenges subsided as his reputation grew. Others soon learned that trying to take the corner from "that tough little Jewish kid" was futile and they stayed away. Danny's newspaper business flourished as did his reputation.

For the next few years, life settled in and Danny became more like his American schoolmates. He studied diligently, attended synagogue, and worked hard both at home and at selling newspapers. During this time he and Jack were close companions. Danny tried to imitate his older brother in whatever he did. Jack was very protective of Danny and tried to steer him away from trouble and encouraged him to study hard so that he would be able to make something of himself.

So, when Jack decided he wanted to try boxing, Danny was not far behind. After all, the Joseph brothers seemed destined to try their lot in the ring. Samuel, the oldest brother, gave boxing a go when his haberdashery business languished. Newspaper accounts read that Sam "showed signs of becoming a top notch middleweight" until he broke his hand in the ring, never regained enough strength in it, and was forced to retire. Brother Dave was a featherweight when the war broke out, but he opted to join the army instead of pursuing a boxing career. When he returned from the war he, too, sustained injuries that prevented his return to the ring.

Jack soon followed in his older brothers' footsteps and started working out at a local boxing gymnasium. Danny frequently accompanied Jack to the gym when he wasn't selling newspapers. Danny would carry Jack's bag, keep time, and act as a corner man as Jack worked out. One day when Jack got ready to work out, Danny couldn't be found. After a search of the gymnasium, Danny was found going through the paces in his brother's togs. Soon, Jack bought his little brother tights, shoes, gloves, and other necessary equipment of his own. Now there were two fighting members of the Joseph family.

Danny Joseph at age ten

A BOXING LIFE BEGINS

And so, at the tender age of sixteen, Danny began his ring career. Danny idolized his brother Jack and whenever possible worked out by his side. In the beginning, Danny spent his time in the gym punching the workout bag, jumping rope, and shadow boxing by himself.

But one day, after badgering his brother to let him get into the ring, Jack relented. One of the smaller fighters who worked out at the gym on a regular basis called Danny into the ring. It didn't take Danny long to get going, and he immediately bore down and came out swinging wildly pursuing the other fighter. The trained boxer could only laugh at Danny's eagerness. Danny, however, was serious. He kept pounding away at the other man who was content just to let him land his punches. When one of Danny's punches landed squarely on the surprised fighter's jaw, it staggered him. That didn't sit too well with the experienced boxer who promptly punched Danny in the nose and sent him to the canvas. Danny had received his first boxing lesson.

Soon Danny was catching the eye of those in the know. Danny's sparring got progressively better under Jack's tutelage, and Danny, more frequently, was allowed to act as a sparring partner for the other young fighters who trained at the gym. As Danny's confidence grew, he also became more aggressive, causing others training in the gym to complain to the gymnasium proprietor, Benny Haskell.

Haskell was not only the boxing establishment's proprietor, but he also served as the manager for several of the fighters who trained there including Danny's brother, Jack. Probably Haskell's best known protégé was heavyweight contender, Fred Fulton. Fulton had been considered a close rival to the then heavyweight champion Jess Willard. However, when a proposed match with Willard fell through, Fulton took on a match with the then little known Jack Dempsey. Dempsey knocked Fulton out in the first round. That was the end of Fulton's championship dreams and the beginning of Dempsey's rise to become heavyweight champion of the world.

As Danny's feistiness grew, Haskell began to pay more attention to the little firebrand. Haskell liked what he saw and began to train Danny in earnest. It wasn't long before Danny abandoned his role as a sparring partner for others and became one of the "boys."

Haskell began to spend a considerable amount of time with little Danny and the newcomer soon became the envy of the others in the gym. While they resented Haskell spending so much time with Danny, they admired his abilities. Danny was a natural in the ring. His style was straightforward and relentless. Jack, however, didn't let the others pester Danny and soon they backed off. Danny trained religiously and his fellow boxers were so taken by his work ethic and talent that it wasn't long before annoyance turned to admiration.

Meanwhile, back at home, Danny's newfound boxing interests caused some consternation. Danny was spending long hours at the gym, just like his brother Jack, but he was beginning to neglect his studies. In addition, his parents were concerned that his synagogue attendance was becoming more infrequent. Nathan and Eva, however, were supportive of Danny, as they were of all the boys.

The war in Europe ended and David came back home to his family. Samuel was married and Jack's own boxing career was progressing handsomely. Danny's love of the ring only grew.

Eventually, he dropped out of school altogether and began training in earnest at the gym.

Haskell wanted to bring along his wunderkind slowly, so he set up a series of exhibition matches with young upstarts from some of the other local gyms. One by one, Danny took care of each opponent that stepped into the ring. Both Benny and Jack were anxious to see how he would do against stronger competition, but were cautious because of Danny's lack of experience. He'd performed well against other boys roughly his own age with similar experience. However, how would he do against someone with honed boxing skills?

Haskell finally decided to give Danny his first test. He'd heard about a boy at another gym who was also showing signs of promise. Haskell contacted the manager of the other gym and set up an exhibition match against the boy. The boys were similar in build, but the other boy had a decided height advantage. Haskell was concerned that the other boy's height and reach would make it very difficult for Danny to land punches. When the bell rang, Danny barreled forward toward the boy. With his body crouched and lunging forward, Danny began throwing punches with reckless abandon. Every one of them landed to the midsection of the other boy. When the boy dropped his arms, instinctively, Danny landed a roundhouse punch to the jaw and the boy went down in a heap. Both managers agreed that the fight should stop immediately to protect the other boy.

The manager told Haskell, "You've got quite a dandy there Benny." From that point forward, Danny was frequently called Dandy Danny. Soon everyone simply called him Dandy.

Haskell was dumbfounded. He knew his boy had talent but he hadn't seen somebody like Danny in a long time. Danny's style took most of those he fought off guard not expecting the smaller boy to be so aggressive. He began to think that perhaps the time had come to give Danny a shot at a professional fight.

Haskell decided to meet with Danny's parents to broach the idea with them. Nathan and Eva knew that fighting was in the boy's blood. All of their sons had been drawn to the ring. Growing up in Grigoriopol had exposed them to violence, and had taught them to fend for themselves. It seemed only natural that boxing would come easy to them. Both Jack and Danny had been "newsies" honing their skills on the streets of Minneapolis, defending their turf selling newspapers. After careful consideration, Nathan gave his blessing to Benny Haskell allowing his sixteen-year-old son, Danny, to step into the ring as a professional prizefighter.

By the time the decision was made for Danny to have his first professional fight, he had already stepped into the ring nearly forty times against other boys with the same dream of becoming a champion boxer. Every one of those boys met defeat at Danny's hands.

By the end of 1919, Benny Haskell had made preparations for Danny to make his professional debut. Jack suggested that Danny come up with a new name to avoid confusion with him. Haskell told Jack that Danny's build and style reminded me of another fighter of the era, Jack Dillon. It was at this point that Dandy Dillon, professional boxer, was born.

BOXING BROTHERS PUTTING MINNEAPOLIS ON FISTIC MAP

LEFT TO RIGHT—JACK JOSEPHS, BENNY HASKELL. MANAGER: DANDY DILLON.

A DANDY BEGINNING

The state of Minnesota played an early and significant role in the development of the sport of boxing in the United States. Some of the country's best fighters, including legendary heavyweight champion John L. Sullivan, fought in Minnesota.

In 1890, the state passed a statute that banned prizefighting, but it was generally ignored. The Governor, William R. Merriam, reluctantly stopped a match between Bob Fitzsimmons and Jim Hill after he was threatened with impeachment. In 1891, the state legislature passed a law which made prizefighting a felony. Boxing remained illegal in Minnesota for the next twenty-three years. George A. Barton, a former referee and sportswriter in Minnesota for over fifty years, wrote in his autobiography, "My Lifetime In Sports", that the passage of that bill led to "sneak fights" that were held in tiny gyms in Minneapolis and St. Paul, as well as barns along the Mississippi and St. Croix rivers.

Eventually, in 1915, boxing became legal again and the state was the locale of many big name fights such as the March 27, 1925, bout when American lightweight champion Gene Tunney defeated world middleweight champion Harry Greb at the St. Paul Auditorium in a bout refereed by George Barton.

In the early days of boxing in the twentieth century, some state laws prohibited a decision in a boxing match if both fighters were still standing at the conclusion of a fight and there was no knockout. However, the common practice was that a pool of ringside reporters would decide among themselves who the winner was and print it in their respective newspapers. These were called "newspaper decisions." That often led to confusion as to who really "won" a particular fight when reporting accounts differed from newspaper to newspaper.

Benny didn't have a tough time narrowing down an opponent for Dandy's first bout. Frankie Gilman was another local fighter who was just starting out himself. This was the perfect match for Dandy, someone with little experience. Because both Dandy and Frankie Gilman were Minneapolis boys, the fight was staged by the Minneapolis Boxing Club at the Mark Hamilton Post of the American Legion at the St. Anthony Commercial Club the first week in January, 1920.

The main event that evening was between local rivals Gus Bloomberg and Dandy's brother, Jack Josephs. They battled to a six-round draw.

While Dandy's fight was no more than a footnote on the boxing card that Saturday evening of January 3, Dandy rang in the new year in grand fashion. The scheduled four-round bantamweight bout was the first fight on the card and Dandy was as anxious as ever to set foot into the ring. George Barton, the sporting editor of the *Minneapolis Daily News* at the time, was the referee for the evening's fight card.

Dandy entered the ring with a large crowd filling the auditorium. As the bell rang for the first round, Dandy came out in typical fashion with his head down, charging forward. Although Gilman was a novice, he had also trained hard for the match. Dandy landed punches quickly and frequently, but Gilman stayed with him. Local reporter, Bill Biff, said in his report that the match "bristled with action…it was almost impossible to follow the punches, let alone keep an accurate account of them." Gilman punched hard but wildly.

The first three rounds were full of action as Dandy pressed the issue with Gilman forcing him to retreat into corners to cover up. By the time the fourth round bell had rung, Dandy was beginning to run out of gas. Up until now, Dandy's fights had been much more controlled. Now, Dandy was trying to prove his worth and was swinging non-stop. Gilman wasn't landing any punches, but Dandy's arms were tiring from his relentless pace. The last round slowed significantly, but the damage had been done. Gilman could never mount any kind of offensive charge and Dandy danced the final round fending off Gilman's weakening punches.

As the bell rang at the end of the fourth and final round, Dandy was exhausted. He also wasn't quite sure what to expect. Did he do enough? The ringside pool of reporters was unanimous in their conclusion awarding Dandy the decision. Dandy Dillon had won his first boxing match.

Following this first bout, Dandy got very little rest. A little more than two weeks later, Dandy found himself in the ring again against Jimmy Valentine of Duluth, Minnesota. Haskell didn't want too much time to lapse between fights so he hurried Dandy back into the ring. It again proved successful. He easily defeated Valentine. Newspapers reported that "he won every round" of the six-round match, which included a roundhouse right hand that sent his opponent to the canvass in the second round. Two fights, two victories.

The next outing for Dandy didn't happen until three months later, in May, when he would meet Percy Buzza in Ontario, Canada. Little did Dandy know at the time, but this bout would be a preview of a second fight he would have with Buzza later in the year. Danny also had another first with this bout, which was that it was the main event for the Winnipeg Attraction Club's fight card. The newspaper called the fight "the sensational fight on the card." The match was hard fought, but Dandy was up to the task, and was able to last ten rounds and score the referee's decision. Both Dandy and Benny were extremely pleased with this outing as it proved that Dandy had the stamina to last in longer fights. Dandy had now upped his record to 3-0.

Dandy fought only twice in the next two months. On June 25, 1920, he faced Al Norton at Nicolette Park, Minnesota. Dandy easily won that four-round opening bout. His next match met with equal success when he defeated Young Mendo in a ten-round match in Buffalo, New York. Benny couldn't make the trip to New York, so he gave the task of watching over his young boxer to Fred Fulton. So Dandy remained undefeated after his first five professional bouts with his record standing at five wins.

Dandy Dillon was a professional boxer, but he was hardly making a comfortable living. Benny Haskell merely provided $50 for each of his bouts after expenses. However, since Dandy had just turned seventeen on July 14, 1920, the money was sufficient. He was still living at home with his parents and Jack, so he didn't need much money. In his next bout, he fought to a ten-round draw with Benny Vogel in Rochester, Minnesota, making this the first blemish on Dandy's record.

To earn extra money that day, Dandy sold copies of *The Boxing Blade* to the crowd before and after his fight reminiscent of his newspaper days. But Dandy was convinced that the bigger paydays were just ahead. His confidence in the ring was growing with each fight, and he was sure he would make more money when he was allowed to fight the bigger names in the game.

A COMING CHAMPION

On September 3, 1920, Dandy was to experience another first in his boxing career and a portend for things to come. He was paired with St. Paul fighter, Johnny Ecklund, in a Nicollet Park fight in an outdoor match. Dandy made short work of Ecklund. He floored him in the first round with a roundhouse right causing Ecklund's eye to close up. In the second round Dandy uncorked a barrage of punches that all landed on the staggered fighter's face keeping him running around the ring until the referee stopped the fight. Dandy had the first knockout of his short career and his record now stood at six victories and one draw.

Dandy's early successes in the ring had many in the know talking. "Was he really that good?", "has he fought anybody that really can test his talent?" were just a couple of the questions that were being asked. Haskell decided that he had to step up the quality of the opposition if Dandy was to be taken seriously and given the opportunity to prove that his talents were worthy of the praise that they were receiving. Before the Ecklund fight, Haskell had already scheduled such a fight, which would test Dandy's skills. Just three days later on September 6, Dandy was to get his chance to prove himself. Dandy was matched against Battling Baker of Glasgow, Scotland, the flyweight champion of Scotland, in a Labor Day contest in Duluth.

Newspaper accounts of Baker described him as "…one of the greatest little fighters developed in the British Isles in many years." He had defeated every good flyweight and bantamweight in Great Britain. Baker was so good that he would work out with local lightweights and heavier boys in preparation for fights. As good of a fighter as Baker was, he was also very shy and would "blush and stammer like a schoolgirl" when you would talk to him.

Blush and stammer is what Baker did. As the bell rang at the start of the bout, Dandy started in usual fashion boring forward and punching with reckless abandon. Baker was caught off guard immediately and began retreating. Dandy's relentless style evidently was something that Baker was not used to. Baker retreated trying to fend off Dillon's attack, but to no avail. When the bell rang at the end of the first round not only was Baker stunned but so was the audience. They expected a tough fight from upstart Dillon, but they were not expecting his early aggressiveness in the match.

The bell sounded for the second round and Dandy came out punching again. This time, as Baker began his retreat, Dandy stepped up the pace. Dandy bobbed and weaved landing body punches to Baker's midsection. Then, out of nowhere, Dandy let go with one of his trademark roundhouse rights that landed squarely on Baker's jaw. Baker went down in a heap. Dillon sought out a neutral corner as the referee started his count. Baker didn't budge. As the count neared closer to ten, Dandy started jumping up and down. As the referee said "ten, you're out" Dandy's jumping had become uncontrollable. He had just defeated the flyweight champion of Scotland. He also scored his second consecutive knockout and improving his record to seven wins without a defeat.

While Dandy was achieving success, his brother Jack was having mixed results. Jack had defeated Gus Bloomberg in a ten-round decision in March, but then suffered three losses in row; once to Johnny Shauer, and twice to Bobby Ward. This troubled Dandy greatly. Although he was happy for himself, he worried about Jack.

Benny Haskell knew that Jack's defeats were having an effect on Dandy and tried to explain to him that fighters simply went though slumps just like baseball players. Even Jack tried to tell Dandy not to worry, explaining that all three loses were close decisions, which could have easily gone his way. Jack's words seemed to help.

After the Baker fight, Dandy was anxious to get back into the ring. If nothing else, he figured, it would take his mind off Jack's run of bad luck. He next took on Jimmy Kelly in La Suer, Minnesota on September 17. Again, Dandy proved that he was the superior boxer. After boxing evenly with Kelly for the first two rounds, Dandy exploded with a barrage of blows that landed heavily on Kelly sending him to the canvas in the third round. Kelly didn't get up giving Dandy his third consecutive knockout.

Dandy was now convinced he was good enough to earn a title fight. Even though he only had nine professional fights under his belt, Dandy's record was impressive. He had eight victories without a defeat and he had scored an impressive string of three knockouts. Dandy asked Benny Haskell to try and get him a fight against Frankie Mason, the American flyweight champion. Benny tried to explain to Dandy that it was still too soon for a fight of that caliber, but Dandy kept asking. To quiet him down, Haskell told him he would try, but first he had to get a few more bouts on his record.

Dandy was touting himself to newspaper reporters as the "Hebrew champion of America." This was quite a statement given Dandy's relatively recent entry into the sport, especially since the number of Jewish fighters was rather significant. But Dandy Danny was feeling his oats. His successes were giving him extraordinary confidence, which did not go unnoticed by Benny Haskell.

In mid-October, Dandy had a rematch with Benny Vogel. Back in August, he and Vogel fought a ten-round draw. The result this time was no different, except that now they only fought a six-round match.

The draw with Vogel did nothing to thwart Dandy's confidence. He was casting a covetous eye on the flyweight title. Next on Danny's agenda was a bout with another well known fighter, Kewpie Callender.

Callender, whose given name was Jimmy Callahan, brought an impressive record into their November match. Callender had whipped some impressive boys by the time he and Dandy were paired up, including beating Benny Vogel back in July. This match was a lively ten-round bout that also ended in a draw. Dandy's frustration with the newspapers was beginning to show following this bout. Also, he and Benny were also beginning to have disagreements about money and whom he was fighting.

It didn't help matters when a couple of weeks later he fought Stewart McLean to a ten-round draw. Tension was starting to build between Dandy and Benny and was also spilling over to Benny's relationship with Jack.

With three consecutive no-decisions for Dandy following an impressive string of victories, including the three consecutive knockouts, the roles reversed between Danny and Jack. Now it was Danny who was frustrated and Jack who was on a winning streak. Jack had won four fights in a row while Dandy's draw streak went on.

Benny sensed that he was losing control of both of his fighters, so he decided to find a big match for Dandy. He found that match in Percy Buzza.

MINNEAPOLIS BANTAM HERE FOR BUZZA BOUT

DANDY DILLON

This clever Minneapolis youth, packing about 114 pounds of boxing machinery, arrived in Winnipeg Monday. He will stack up against Percy Buzza, the Winnipeg boy, Wednesday evening in a ten three-minute round contest. This will be the main boxing bout on the Winnipeg Attraction club's all-star card which has as its feature a match between John Albrecht and Tom Johnstone for the police wrestling championship of the American continent.

CHAMPION!

Dandy had fought, and beaten, Percy Buzza earlier in the year, but now Buzza was the flyweight champion of Canada. Dandy had already beaten one champion, Battling Baker, when he was flyweight champion of Scotland. But in boxing circles, this was considered a more impressive bout for Dandy. Minnesota's close proximity to the Canadian border gave more visibility and credibility to the Canadian fighters.

The fight was scheduled for December 8, 1920, at the Board of Trade Building, a little less than a year since Dandy entered the boxing arena as a professional prizefighter. In that short period of time, Dandy had impressed the crowds and backed it up with impressive victories in the ring. He had twelve professional fights by the time he traveled to Winnipeg, Canada for his match with Buzza. Although his last three fights had ended in draws, Dandy carried a ring record of eight wins, four draws, and no defeats into the bout.

Jack accompanied his little brother to Winnipeg to act as his corner man and to instill him with confidence. In addition, Jack acted as a go-between for his brother and Benny Haskell. Jack didn't want any distractions for Dandy entering the fight. At seventeen years of age, Dandy was still a boy, even though it seemed like, in the past year, he had grown immensely.

Dandy's confidence was already high as he prepared for the fight. As he read his own press clippings it got even higher. A local Winnipeg newspaper reporter wrote prior to the scheduled match:

> "That Percy Buzza has a real battle on his hands for December 8 when he stacks up against Dandy Dillon, of Minneapolis in a ten-round go at the Board of Trade building is apparent from Dillon's record during the past 12 months. Dillon is a fellow much the same build as Buzza, who possesses a knockout blow. Dandy has put three opponents to sleep."

Buzza was still upset about the results of the first match they had. He felt that he had won, but the referee and judges saw it much differently. This dispute was a main reason why the Winnipeg Attraction Club decided that the two should meet again to settle the score. The card that evening in Winnipeg was a combination of wrestling bouts and boxing matches. Although the wrestling matches were entertaining, it was the boxing end of the show that was worth the price of admission.

Dandy had both a reach and weight advantage over Buzza, outweighing his opponent by five pounds. When the fight began, it was apparent that the Canadian crowd backed their man over Dillon. Whenever Buzza landed a blow, no matter how insignificant its damage, the crowd roared with approval. Over the first eight rounds, the two pugilists traded blows with Dandy's causing much more damage. Buzza fought gamely and heroically against Dillon.

Buzza was weak by the time the ninth round opened. And, as one newspaper report put it, "Dillon is a great piece of fighting machinery. He stood up to his man all the way, used a left jab to advantage and had a quick shift and wicked right upper-cut which meted out damage." The "Hebrew champion of America" had the much better of the battle. He floored Buzza in the eighth round with a smashing right to the jaw and it didn't appear that Buzza would make it through the ninth round.

The gong had barely sounded when Dandy went after Buzza in the ninth. Dandy landed a hard right to Buzza's chest who went down with a thud. Percy Buzza, the Canadian Flyweight Champion, lay sprawled on the canvas of the boxing ring at the Board of Trade Building in Winnipeg, Manitoba, Canada, victim of a crushing right hand to the heart by Dandy Dillon. The match had been controlled by Dillon from the outset and when he landed his vicious blow to Buzza's chest after fifty-six seconds of the ninth round, the seventeen-year-old Russian Jewish immigrant became the undefeated Flyweight Champion of Canada in only his thirteenth bout as a professional boxer. On December 8, 1920, after thirteen fights, including four knockouts and a record of nine wins and four draws, Moishe Josofsky achieved something he never imagined growing up in Czarist Russia, a boxing championship.

The knockout was not so much the result of the blow delivered in the ninth, as it was sheer exhaustion due to the shock sustained at the end of the eighth. Buzza fought gamely, but he was no match for Dandy Dillon.

Jack jumped over the ropes to get into the ring, closely followed by Benny Haskell. Dandy had gone over to check on Buzza and was bear-hugged from behind by his brother. The three of them hugged and hollered, and hugged and hollered again.

Dandy Dillon, Flyweight Champion of Canada

DILLON VS MASON

Frankie Mason was the American flyweight champion in 1921 with an impressive ring record. By that time he was thirty-one years old and had over sixty victories in the ring under his belt. During his illustrious career, he had over two hundred fights. In 1919 alone, he fought forty-two times. One of those fights was a 12-round draw with Joe Lynch who would go on to be the bantamweight champion of the world.

Dandy was the newly crowned flyweight champion of Canada, but he wanted to be America's champion. Frankie Mason stood in the way of that goal. Dandy wanted a fight with Mason in the worst way, and begged his manager to get him a fight. Haskell tried, but was unable to work Dandy into Mason's busy fight schedule.

Instead, Dandy had to settle for another fight with Jimmy Valentine on January 21, 1921, in Duluth, Minnesota. Dandy had been fighting professionally for a year now and although was considered by many to be a veteran fighter, Danny was still only seventeen years old.

The fight with Valentine was a late decision. Valentine was scheduled to fight Van Cushing, but Cushing was unable to make the bout. Dandy substituted for Cushing and met Valentine in an eight-round bout. Valentine was again no match for Dandy. Although the fight was a lively one, Dandy landed punches almost at will and outscored his opponent two-to-one to win the newspaper decision.

Dandy was convinced that his 10-0-4 record now deserved him a shot at Mason's title. Little did he know that the fight would come much sooner than he thought.

Frankie Mason, who fought out of Ft. Wayne, Indiana, was scheduled to meet Chicago Bantamweight Johnny Ritchie in a ten-round match on February 22. Just two days before the match, though, Richie was finishing up training and broke his hand while sparring with his partner. The local promoter frantically sent out telegrams to all of the good 112- to 118-pound fighters in the section. Benny Haskell responded immediately that his boy was ready to go and would take the earliest train to Des Moines for the bout. The Des Moines Athletic Club was elated at the idea of the match between the two champions and quickly agreed to the substitution.

Although Dandy was anxious for the fight, he worried that he wasn't in the best of condition. This was because, after the Valentine match, Dandy took a much needed rest and stayed away from the gym. So when the fight opportunity with Mason came with only one day's notice, Dandy had not trained in over two weeks.

Mason was a local favorite and had the crowd behind him at the Auditorium in Des Moines. When the fight began, Dandy started in his usual fashion, leading the action. But Mason was the general in the ring. He refused to take the lead and let Dillon press the action letting him swing away and then countered when the young Minnesotan missed.

Dandy had the better long range work and used his left jab efficiently to Mason's midsection. But the American champion was either going away as the punch landed or turned his body in such a way as not to absorb the full impact of the punch. Dandy was frustrated. He couldn't land a single punch to Mason's face during the entire bout.

The fifth, ninth, and tenth rounds saw lots of action, but again Dandy's swings were missing the mark or had little impact on the much more experienced fighter. At the end of the fifth, Mason caught Dandy on the chin with a right, which left him staggering against the ropes.

The ninth round had several fine exchanges and Dillon landed a straight left to Mason's chest and one to his stomach. However, Mason came back with a right and left to Dandy's chin. At the beginning of the tenth round, Dandy rushed Mason in an effort to score big. Mason was too skilled for Dandy. He avoided most of Dandy's swings and when the ten-round match concluded, there was little doubt who had won. Mason had outpointed Dandy and handed the young boxer his first taste of defeat in the ring.

Dandy was pretty down in the dumps after the fight. It was fortuitous that his brother Jack had come back from his doldrums to be able to give Dandy the support he needed. Dandy felt he simply wasn't prepared for the bout. As much as he wanted the fight, he knew that he hadn't properly trained for it. But when the opportunity presented itself, he wasn't about to turn it down. Almost immediately he wanted a rematch with Mason.

Instead, Dandy took a week off after the Mason fight and then headed back to the gymnasium to begin training again. He was determined to never be ill-prepared again going into a fight. Soon, he was anxious to get back into the ring.

Dandy travelled to Detroit, Michigan, for his next fight on March 14. He was scheduled to fight Eddie White in a ten-rounder. White was another experienced boxer who had been fighting since 1916. Dandy figured that fighting another boxer with the type of experience that Mason had would help if and when they ever fought again.

The fight with White was just what the doctor ordered. Dandy was sharp again as he pummeled White for ten rounds sending White to the canvas in the seventh round. Dandy won the decision decisively and upped his record to 11-1-4.

Jack Josephs was on his own winning streak. Dandy's loss to Frankie Mason seemed not only to rile Dandy, but it also seemed to invigorate Jack. Jack fought three times after the Mason fight with two victories and a draw. So, after Jack's three fight losing streak, he was now riding a streak that saw seven victories and one draw in his last eight fights. Jack's victories also helped Dandy. They appeared to feed on each other's successes.

Haskell's next foe for Dandy took the form of Frankie Jummati. Jummati was another Chicagoan that the Cedar Rapids Athletic Club felt was worthy to meet Dandy in the main event on April 29. The Italian Jumatti had earned a reputation as being one of the hardest workers in the ring, but he was also a journeyman. While he didn't shy away from a tough fight, he seldom walked away with a victory. To his credit, he had fought Frankie Mason on four occasions. Unfortunately, he walked away empty handed each time. The best he could do was a draw.

Dandy was at his finest for this bout with Jummati. Jummati lived up to his billing as a hard hitter, but he was no match for Dandy's speed and cleverness. Jummati swung hard and frequently, but he missed connecting as Dandy dodged blows aimed at his head and countered with wicked blows to the body in return. When all was said and done, Dandy had defeated the Chicago bantamweight in each round of the ten-round match. One newspaper reported that Dandy "made a chopping block of Frankie Jummati for ten consecutive rounds." The most that could be said for Jummati was that he withstood Dandy's punishment for the entire ten rounds.

With Dandy's record now standing at 12-1-4, he was itching for that rematch with Frankie Mason. Haskell had been trying to get the rematch since the Dillon-Mason bout in February. His wishes for that rematch were finally answered when Mason agreed to meet

Dillon for a second time in the middle of May. In a letter to the *Cedar Rapids Evening Times*, Haskell told the newspaper of Mason's acceptance of the rematch at the request of the Cedar Rapids Athletic Club.

The local baseball association approached Alex Fidler, matchmaker at the athletic club to stage the bout on opening day of the local baseball season. Initially, the Mason camp was looking to stage a fight with Babe Asher of St. Louis. However, Iowa State Athletic Club promoter, "Snapper" Kennedy, yielded to pressure from the Cedar Rapids club that Dillon be on the bill. Much of that pressure came as a result of Dandy's trouncing of Jummati, which made a lasting impression on the local fight fans. He had made such a hit that local fans were clamoring for Dillon to be brought back.

Dandy took a few days off after the Jummati fight but began training in earnest when Haskell gave him the news. Dandy was determined to be at his best when he fought Mason again. Mason told the newspapers that he was in the best shape of his career and would be in "tip-top form when he tangles with the slashing bantam from Minnesota."

Leading up to the May 16 bout, the newspapers were having a field day promoting the fight. Earl Coughlin of the *Cedar Rapids Evening Times* wrote that "When Frankie Mason, claimant of the flyweight title, steps into the ring here to do battle with Dandy Dillon on the night of May 16, fistic fans in this neighborhood will be privileged to see not only a truly wonderful ringman, but one of the greatest fighting machines, for his inches, ever assembled."

Coughlin called Dillon "that young tiger from Minneapolis" and assured boxing fans that he would bring out the best in Mason. Mason was being built up as indestructible. But Dandy would hear nothing of it. He was sure that he had the skills and the determination to finally beat Mason at his own game.

Despite Mason's brilliant achievements in the ring, many in boxing circles were of the opinion that Dillon was just the type of fighter who could beat Mason. The beating that Dandy gave Jummati was still fresh in the minds of the locals, including the boxing media. Coughlin was one of those who thought Dandy just might have a chance. "When he crawls through the ropes to face Mason," Coughlin wrote, "There will be many at the ringside who sincerely believe him fully capable of vanquishing the veteran."

Frankie Mason respected Dillon's abilities. Although he had defeated him three months earlier with relative ease, he knew that Dandy had not been at the top of his game when they fought.

After Mason had agreed to come to Cedar Rapids for a bout on May 16, without knowing who his opponent would be, he quickly asked for a later date when he was advised that the Twin City star was to be his foe. Mason sent a telegram to the promoters insisting that Dillon's weight not be one ounce over 118 pounds by 3:00 p.m. on fight day. Mason only weighed 110 pounds and he didn't want to give too much away to the Minnesotan. Haskell assured Fidler that Dandy was already at the required weight. Mason didn't fear Dandy, but he simply wanted to be sure he would have ample time to train and be at his best.

Dandy's training regimen for the bout consisted of a five mile run each morning, and boxing between eight to twelve rounds with his brother Jack and another sparring partner named Eddie Deboy. He chose Deboy because he was extremely fast and Dandy wanted to be prepared for Mason's quickness. Dandy had never trained this conscientiously for a bout before, but he was intent on being in his best shape ever.

May 16 was a big day in Cedar Rapids from a local sporting standpoint. The day began with a parade, with other festivities following. In the afternoon, the season opening baseball game between Bunnyville and Bloomington was held. The evening was capped with four boxing matches highlighted by the main event between American Flyweight Champion Frankie Mason and Canadian Flyweight Champion Dandy Dillon.

Anticipation ran high when the two combatants stepped into the ring that Monday evening. The only disappointment was that at the weigh-in, earlier in the day, Dandy tipped the scales heavier than expected. As a result, the fight was not sanctioned as a flyweight bout and Mason's American title was not in jeopardy.

The crowd was already pumped up from the earlier bouts and was ready for the main event. Both Mason and Dillon had trained hard and were prepared for the fight. There would be no excuses for either's performance this time.

When the bell sounded for the first round Dandy started out in his typical manner. He barreled forward with his head down. Intent on carrying the fight from the outset, Dandy started the fight in the same fashion as he did against Frankie Jummati. He took the lead by driving his left to Mason's stomach with considerable power and immediately had Mason on the defensive. Dandy was the aggressor throughout the first round scoring with a series of body punches. In the second round, Dandy again landed a left to Mason's midsection but Mason responded with a right and a left to Dillon's head in return. But Dandy continued to bore forward and chased Mason relentlessly around the ring until the bell rang.

In the third, Dandy began by landing a left jab to Mason's nose followed with a hard right to the American champion's mouth. He continued to use his left on Mason's body effectively while avoiding Mason's counter-punches. Just before the bell rang at the conclusion of the round, Mason landed his best punch yet, a hard left to the Dillon's chin.

The fourth round found both fighters holding back and catching their breath. The action had been non-stop up to this point and each needed to regroup. Neither boxer landed many punches. In the fifth round Dandy was the aggressor once again. The two fighters worked close and tangled up until Dillon broke away with a right cross to the jaw and a hard left to the body, which jarred Mason all over.

Mason tried his best to overcome Dillon's strong fifth by taking the fight to Dandy. Dandy, however, showed Mason his defensive skills by making him swing wildly, ducking under Mason's hard swings. Coming out of their corners in the seventh round, Dandy worked Mason into the ropes and used both hands to score points to his opponent's head. After a clinch that had both fighters again trying to catch their breath, Dillon landed a hard right to Mason's jaw, followed by a Mason left to Dillon's mouth.

The final three rounds saw Mason come to the realization that he was being beaten by his younger opponent. Accordingly, he tried to take the offensive. But every time he tried to mount an attack, Dandy was ready for him. Dandy was tiring, but he had enough left in the tank to ward off any serious attack by Mason.

When the bell sounded at the conclusion of the tenth round, Dandy knew he was vindicated. He had beaten his foe in each round of the match and had whipped the crafty ring veteran.

Almost immediately after the fight, the local boxing writers were calling for a match between Dandy and world champion Joe Lynch.

LOCAL FIGHTERS TO INVADE EASTERN RINGS THIS FALL

STANDING, LEFT TO RIGHT—DANDY DILLON, JACK JOSEPHS, FRED FULTON. SITTING—BENNY HASKELL.

THE VETERAN FIGHTER

Dandy was jubilant after whipping Frankie Mason. He now felt that he had earned the respect of the boxing world and had the record to prove it. After defeating Mason, Dandy had upped his ring record to 13 wins and four draws with only one defeat. By the tender age of nineteen, he had defeated both the American and Canadian flyweight champions, as well as other top notch fighters in the game.

Despite his high spirits, Dandy was starting to feel tired. In the span of less than eighteen months, Dandy had gone from a sixteen-year-old novice to a grizzled veteran of eighteen fights. Averaging a fight a month took its toll on the young nineteen-year-old veteran. Wanting to bask in the glory of his recent victory, Dandy took the next two months off before stepping into the ring again.

Jack Josephs was also continuing his winning ways. He won another three fights in a row and now had a string of ten consecutive fights without a loss. The Joseph brothers were flying high. Jack was equally as happy for Dandy's successes as he was of his own and he also wanted a break from the ring.

For their well-earned break, Dandy and Jack went home to Minneapolis shortly after Dandy's victory over Frankie Mason. They simply yearned for the comforts of home before starting up in the ring again. Dandy and Jack were both making good money. Now they wanted to spend a little of it, and savor the good life. So, at home they relax, go to the movies, and enjoy the company of their family, all those things they hadn't had the time for.

While the Joseph boys were having a good time at home, Benny Haskell wasn't pleased. He wanted both boys to get back to training and back into the ring. After all, if the boys didn't make money, neither did he.

Benny finally convinced Dandy that it was time to get back into the ring and scheduled an Independence Day bout with Ray Rose in Butte, Montana. Rose had a reputation as a hard hitter and carried an impressive knockout record into the fight. Billed as the "Bantam with the T.N.T. Punch" he was from Portland, Oregon, with most of his success out west.

The July 4, 1921, fight card advertised itself as a double main event. In addition to the Dillon v Rose match, Dave Shade was scheduled to fight Joe Simonich in a welterweight bout. The boxing show, to be held at the Broadway Theater under the auspices of the American Legion, was having a tough time getting its due. On July 2, Jack Dempsey was fighting Georges Carpentier in what was to be the first fight broadcast by radiophone. So, the local media did whatever they could to drum up the event.

Despite the fact that Dandy's reputation was growing and Rose's knockout record was impressive, most boxing fans were interested in the Dempsey bout. However, the Butte fans filled the arena for America's birthday.

While the fireworks were going on outside, there wasn't much in store for the fight crowd that evening. In a lackluster performance, partially attributed to Dandy's general lack of interest in the fight, Rose and Dillon fought to a fifteen-round draw. Rose carried the fight in the first ten rounds, but was unable to put Dandy away. In the final five rounds, Dandy moved in and forced the fight by frequently scoring jabs and punches. After taking considerable abuse for the first ten rounds, Dillon rallied and became more aggressive. It was on the heels of that late round aggressiveness that Dandy was able to earn a draw.

Perhaps the highlight of the fight came during the thirteenth round. As Rose was breaking away from a clinch, he lifted Dandy off his feet and swung him around. Immediately Benny Haskell tried to climb through the ropes to defend his fighter but was prevented by the referee. Ray Rose's manager, Billy Rose, started for Haskell, but was stopped by ringside spectators. After the fight was over, Billy Rose again caused a disturbance trying to get at Haskell. This time it took not only the referee to stop Rose's manager, but also two policemen. As a result of Rose's manager's actions, he was fined $25 by the boxing commission.

Benny Haskell wasn't happy with Dandy's performance, but neither was Dandy. Dandy's excuse was that he was simply tired. Benny thought, however, that it had more to do with Dandy's lack of commitment and training for the bout. Regardless of the reason, the relationship between Benny and Dandy was starting, again, to show some strain.

Jack and Dandy both were beginning to feel that Benny's interests differed from theirs. Benny had other fighters in his stable, but the brother duo of Jack Josephs and Dandy Dillon had been the best one-two punch that Haskell had.

It would be another four months before Dandy would step into the ring again. Benny was beginning to step away from Dandy's daily training. He let his heavyweight contender, Fred Fulton, take Dandy under his wings instead.

After arriving back in Minneapolis, Dandy and Jack talked between themselves about how much longer to keep Benny as their manager. They concluded that it wouldn't be much longer. In fact, Dandy's next match, scheduled for November 11, 1921, against Benny Mertens, would be his last fight under the tutelage of Benny Haskell.

Coincidentally, November 11, 1921, was the third anniversary of the Armistice that ended the Great War. In October, Congress passed legislation, signed by President Woodrow Wilson, to officially designate a Federal holiday on November 11, as Armistice Day, to honor those that had participated in that war. So, there was a certain irony that Dandy would engage in a prize fight on the very day celebrating the end of fighting.

Fighting in Rochester, Minnesota, Dandy outpointed Benny Mertens to take the ten-round decision that night. Dandy chased his rival all over the ring for the first seven rounds, during which he piled up a big lead. Mertens rallied in the last three rounds, but it was a case of too little too late. The crowd was entertained though, and gave both fighters a big hand as they left the ring.

The Rochester fight was Dandy's last fight of 1921, and he ended his second year as a professional fighter with a record of fourteen wins, five draws, and his one loss, which was later avenged to Frankie Mason.

Dandy decided to remain home with his family for the rest of the year to ponder his future. Although he and Jack had decided to part ways with Benny Haskell, they hadn't told him yet.

The time to tell Benny came shortly after the first of the year. First Jack informed Haskell that he was leaving his management. Shortly afterwards, Dandy told him the same. Haskell felt bad because he had groomed Dandy and Jack, However he also understood that a parting of the ways was probably the best for all. Initially, Haskell took the news in stride because he was still preparing his prized pupil, Fred Fulton, for a title bout with heavyweight champion Jack Dempsey. But Fulton couldn't stand to be all alone in the once thriving Haskell army, so he, too, decided to seek out a new commander. Suddenly, Haskell was a general without an army.

Dandy Dillon Trains for a Fight

A CONFUSING NEW BEGINNING

In January 1922, Dandy, Jack, and Fred Fulton went East for Dandy's next fight. Fulton decided to take Dandy to New York with him to try and get him more exposure on the East Coast. There he linked up with Jack Bulger, a Newark, New Jersey, promoter and boxing manager. He found Dandy's next opponent in Newark, Jimmy Tomasulo, a former amateur champion from Elizabeth, New Jersey. This was a new experience for Dandy who would be making his first fight since leaving the only manager he had known since first lacing up the gloves as a fifteen year old in Benny Haskell's gym.

Fighting primarily as a bantamweight now, since he found it more difficult to keep the pounds off, Dandy gained renown fighting in Minnesota, Iowa, and Canada. However, he was still a virtual unknown in the East. So when he stepped into the ring against Jimmy Tomasulo on January 23, few had high expectations for Dandy. Tomasulo had gained some fame from his amateur days, and was expected to win the bout handily.

When the fight started, Dandy began in his typical fashion, immediately carrying the action to his opponent. From the outset it was apparent that Tomasulo had vastly underestimated his talented foe. Dandy connected in the first round with a right-hand smash that cut Tomasulo's eye. The second round was a repetition of the first as Dandy ripped home blows that further damaged the other fighter. In the third round, Tomasulo bravely fought back and scored with a couple of right hands of his own, which briefly confused Dillon.

In the fourth and fifth rounds, the two boxers traded punches, but Tomasulo started swinging wildly because of the blood flowing into his eye from a first round injury. It took all his skill to escape the round with as little damage as he did.

The eight-round fight ended in much the same way as it began. Dandy scored heavily and Tomasulo boxed defensively. Tomasulo fought gamely, but it was Dandy who came away with a decisive victory. The headline in the local newspaper the next day declared, "Unknown Wonder Defeats Tomasulo."

The New Year began in smart fashion. Dandy had his first victory of the year, and he had accomplished this feat without Benny Haskell as his manager.

Nonetheless, the next few months proved to be difficult for Dandy. First he severely sprained his hand while training. This injury limited his ability to schedule another fight. Also, he was unable to obtain a capable manager to handle his affairs. Fred Fulton served as a temporary "manager" shortly after leaving Benny Haskell, but Dandy needed someone who could handle the administrative chores, such as setting up his fights, and working with him in the gym. Jack helped him too, as much as he could while training. But he, too, needed to find himself a new manager.

There was plenty of speculation, in the press, that Dandy would sign on with Sammy Goldman who had managed Pete Herman to the world bantamweight championship, but that didn't happen. Finally, in May of 1922, Dandy and Jack got their new manager. They placed themselves under the direction of New York manager, Billy McCarney. McCarney was a veteran promoter as well as boxing manager.

Unfortunately, that relationship only lasted for one bout against Eddie Nemo on August 18, in Hibbing, Minnesota. Nemo took the fight with just a few hours notice because the fighter McCarney scheduled, Billy O'Brien of Chicago failed to show. Nemo fought gallantly against Dandy, but finally succumbed to a roundhouse right hand that sent him to the canvas in the ninth round. Nemo never recovered, and Dandy had his first knockout since he laid out Percy Buzza to capture the Canadian flyweight crown nearly two years ago.

While the one-bout marriage with Billy McCarney was a successful one, Dandy wasn't happy that it had taken so long to land a fight. He was even more irritated that it was only because of a last minute substitution the fight come about.

Jack Josephs had more success with McCarney, as he was able to secure four bouts in the same time frame that Dandy had his one. Fortunately for Jack, this relationship resulted in his continuing his unbeaten streak during this period. He won three of the fights and had a draw in the other.

Jack's success, however, didn't stop Dandy from wanting another chance at the top. He quickly parted ways with McCarney and aligned himself with Sol Goldstein, who was able to secure a match for Dandy just a few weeks later.

Dandy and his new manager traveled to Omaha, Nebraska, for a September 4 match with Cyclone Yelsky. Yelsky hailed from Cleveland, Ohio, and didn't have much of a record going into the bout. That proved true when Dandy knocked out his opponent in the first round of the fight. While Dandy's competition wasn't real strong, he was nonetheless happy that his last two fights resulted in knockouts. Coming off his extended layoff, Dandy was happy with his progress.

With Dandy's record now standing at an impressive seventeen wins, five draws, and one loss he was looking for new challenges. He felt that with Sol Goldstein he had a competent manager. Jack also was impressed with Sol, so he too departed the stable of Billy McCarney.

Dandy went back home to Minneapolis following his victory over Yelsky. He wanted to see his parents and brothers and sisters again. It seemed as though he had been on the road for an eternity during the past two and a half years, and he longed for the stability that family offered. At the age of nineteen, Dandy had experienced more than many do in a lifetime. The instability of his management contributed to Dandy's insecurity and he just wanted to be around friendly faces. His brother Jack provided support for Dandy when they traveled on the road together, but, while never admitting it to anyone, he missed the father figure he found in Benny Haskell. Benny had always been there for him right from the beginning. Not having him around was a loss that Dandy never got used to.

After renewing himself at home for a couple of weeks, Sol Goldstein felt the best cure for Dandy's doldrums was to get him back into the ring soon. So he scheduled a fight close to home with Joey Schwartz in St. Paul, for October 9. That fight was just what the doctor ordered as Schwartz challenged Dandy for ten rounds before eventually losing the newspaper decision.

Goldstein was playing it smart with his fighter by not presenting him with too tough of a challenge. He wasn't quite sure yet if Dandy was mentally up to the task of taking on a seasoned fighter. Dandy, however, was insistent that Goldstein get him a quality fight. Tension between fighter and manager heightened to the point where Goldstein had enough and sent Dandy packing.

In less than a year, Dandy was without a manager for the third time. This time Dandy looked closer to home as he sought out a new manager. That man turned out to be Mike Gibbons. Gibbons was a former successful fighter and St. Paul native, who gained renown as the "St. Paul Phantom." Mike was also the brother of Tommy Gibbons who would later fight Jack Dempsey for the heavyweight championship of the world.

Gibbons, a former middleweight, had fought over a hundred times and was thoroughly acquainted with all aspects of the fight game. He quickly took charge of Dandy's affairs and was determined to get the little man back on the right track. Gibbons, being a local, had followed Dandy's career with interest and was sure the lad had what it takes to move further up the championship ladder.

Gibbons wanted to challenge Dandy immediately and set up a bout with Joe Burger. Gibbons had already arranged for one of his other fighters, "Saph" McKenna, to step into the ring against Jack Doyle in Denver, Colorado, on October 27. So, it wasn't difficult to get Dandy on the same card that night in Denver.

Burger had beaten Gibbon's other boy, McKenna, a few weeks earlier and "Phantom" Mike was looking for a little revenge by pairing Dandy against him. Dandy wasn't well known in Denver and Burger was a heavy favorite to beat the Minneapolis lad.

The fight between Dillon and Burger turned out to be one of the most controversial in Dandy's career. Once considered one of the best boxing towns in the West, boxing had been on the wane in Denver for some time. *The Boxing Blade* reported that boxing gates in Denver used to bring in between $5,000 and $15,000 in receipts per fight card. Now they were lucky to bring in $1,000. In addition, *The Blade* said, "...decisions that were lately handed out in Denver...are decisions that a blind man would be ashamed to give."

Sure enough, those concerns surfaced in the Dillon v Burger match. Receipts that evening were only $1,070 with just a handful of people in the audience as the fight began between Denver native Burger and Dandy Dillon.

Dandy, in his customary manner, had forced the action from the beginning of the bout and continued that way throughout the twelve-round fight. Dandy kept Burger on the defensive and nearly had him out on several occasions. Reporters for *The Boxing Blade* were in attendance at the fight and reported that, "at the start of the twelfth and last round, old timers around the ring gave Dillon ten rounds out of the eleven. No matter how the last round went, Dillon would have won by a mile."

In round twelve, Dandy tore after Burger driving him from corner to corner with heavy body blows without Burger putting up much of a defense. Finally, Dandy connected with a hard left to Burger's stomach followed by a hard right to his jaw. Burger was hanging on for dear life. When the bell rang at the finish, *The Blade* reported "Dillon was apparently as fresh as when he started. Burger was a wreck."

When the decision of the judges was handed to the referee, he stood with a shocked stare for a minute. Both judges had given the decision to Burger! There was nothing for the referee to do but to raise Burger's hand.

While the crowd was a small one, they erupted with such fervor one would have thought the house was packed. Cat calls and boos came from the crowd deploring the decision. Considering they were coming from Burger's home crowd, the decision was even more appalling. Burger, who had a reputation for being quite the gentleman, walked over to Dandy, shook his hand and said, "I am sorry boy. They called it wrong, you won."

On the way out of the arena, one of the judges, Ed Lyons, a sports writer for *The Denver Times,* was punched in the face by a spectator. A writer for *The Boxing Blade* reported that an old timer that he spoke with said, "That is why there are no people in the house."

That same writer went back to see how Dandy was taking the decision and found him "crying like a baby" in his dressing room. Dandy told him, "it was my first start in the West and I gave them my best. I know I won by a big margin. Burger admits I beat him. The referee says I won by a mile. Everyone says I won. But the judges say I lost and when I go back home that is what the papers there will say. I don't care if I ever win again. What's the use?"

The next morning one of the promoters of the fight, Jack Kanner, sought out Dillon and told him, "You are one of the greatest little fighters who ever came to Denver. Will you fight Joe Lynch for the title here inside thirty days, and who do you want for a referee?" Dandy quickly agreed, but told Kanner that Lynch could name his own referee.

The next day the following telegram was sent to Eddy Mead, manager of Joe Lynch:

> Eddy Mead, Mgr. of Joe Lynch, Bantamweight Champion of the World, care of Sporting Editor, Morning Telegraph, New York City, New York.
>
> "WILL OFFER YOU AS MY VERY BEST TERMS FORTY PER CENT GROSS AND TRANSPORTATION. JOE LYNCH TO BOX DANDY DILLON TWELVE ROUNDS FOR WORLD TITLE, MY CLUB ANY TIME IN FOUR WEEKS. YOUR OWN REFEREE REPLY."
> (Signed) JACK KANNER.

For whatever reason, however, Mead never responded to Kanner's telegram and Dandy's opportunity to fight for the world championship against Joe Lynch never came to pass. Given the state of affairs of boxing in Denver, it's safe to say that Kanner's offer was never taken seriously. Mead had nothing to gain by staging a championship match in a town that was known for questionable decisions. Additionally, while Dandy Dillon was someone to be reckoned with, Mead saw no advantage to put the championship belt on the line against someone he knew very little about.

Dandy Dillon in Butte, Montana 1923

GO WEST YOUNG MAN

Losing the bout to Joe Burger in the way that it happened was devastating to Dandy. He was thrilled with Jack Kanner's offer to stage a championship fight with Joe Lynch, however, as the days passed with no response from the Lynch camp, Dandy became increasingly disillusioned. For a short time, he even seriously considered hanging up his gloves.

Mike Gibbons did what he could to restore his new young charge's confidence and he escorted Dandy back home to Minneapolis. There Dandy rejoined Jack at the family home and the two spoke about their recent misfortunes. While Dandy lamented the stolen match with Burger, Jack was reeling from three loses, a draw, and a solitary victory on his own West Coast swing.

Jack and Danny talked at length about the possibility of moving out West on a more permanent basis to explore the boxing opportunities out there. While Jack didn't have much success inside the ring, he enjoyed the Pacific Northwest, boxing in Vancouver British Columbia, Seattle and Portland. Jack was convincing, though, and Dandy said he'd be willing to give it a try. Gibbons agreed with the Joseph brothers' decision to try going out West. But first, he scheduled Dandy for a couple of fights in Great Falls, Montana.

Mike Collins, Mike Gibbon's partner, accompanied Dandy to Montana and was to be in his corner for the two fights. Collins also provided reporting duties for *The Boxing Blade* and was busy working on the Christmas edition of *The Boxing Blade.*

In the first fight, Dandy was matched against Butte fighter Sammy Gordon. Gordon, who was the same age as Dandy, as well as Jewish, hailed originally from Portland, Oregon. Gordon was also somewhat of a braggart. When told of Dandy's exploits in the ring, Gordon brushed them off by saying that he had accomplished as much as Dillon on the West Coast. Gordon did, however, have one victory under his belt that escaped Dandy. He had knocked out Ray Rose a few months earlier in Boise. Dandy could only manage a draw with Rose when the two met a year and a half ago.

Dandy arrived early for the December 29 fight so that he could get in some training following his two-day journey from Minnesota. Both Dillon and Gordon had staged Christmas Day workouts, at separate times, for the fans. Both being Jews, it wasn't unusual for either of them to train on that day. Gordon's manager, Paul Bader, said that his fighter was in the best shape of his career and had nothing to fear in Dillon. "I have never seen Sammy going better or hitting harder" he said, "He is due to go into this ring right at the top of his form."

Gordon may have been at the top of his form, but so was Dandy. The scheduled twelve-rounder came to a sudden end when Dandy knocked him out in the ninth round of the main event of the American Legion's holiday card. A slashing exchange between the two boxers in the middle of the ring ended when Dillon drove a left flush to Gordon's jaw and left him stretched out on the canvas floor. Gordon got up on one knee when the referee counted to four and eventually made it to his feet at the count of nine. Dandy had no trouble measuring him for another left to the jaw and Gordon went down in a heap again. He tried to get up at the count of eight but crumpled back to the canvas.

The fight started uneventfully, with the first few rounds amounting to a sparring match. But in the third round, Dandy took charge and began to carry the fight to Gordon. In the sixth, seventh, and eighth rounds it was evident that Gordon was no match for Dandy. Gordon had taken a lot of punishment in those rounds and they finally took their toll when Dandy finished him off in the ninth.

Both Collins and Dandy were pleased with the results of the prizefight. After the Joe Burger debacle, Dandy was ready for an easy fight. Dandy had scored his seventh career knockout and had upped his record to 19-2 with five draws.

Dandy rang in the new year in Butte with his second area bout against Portland native, Lackey Morrow. Morrow was a tall, speedy fighter who fought exclusively in the West. As a consequence, they didn't have any common opponents by which Dandy could measure him. Morrow was a streaky fighter with an impressive record but headed into the match with a four-bout losing streak.

Just seconds into the fight that evening of January 8, the crowd knew that Morrow's losing streak would probably continue. After sparring for just a moment's time, Dandy uncorked a short right hook to Morrow's jaw which sent his lanky body sprawling to the canvas. Morrow popped up quickly, but the tone had been set. For the next nine rounds Dandy was content dancing around the ring occasionally darting forward with a barrage of body blows. Morrow scored a few punches of his own periodically, but Dandy was in charge if not dominating.

In the eleventh round, Dandy once again unloaded a strong right hand to Morrow's jaw opening up a cut inside his mouth causing blood to gush. Morrow gamely hung in with Dandy, and the twelfth round was merely a formality as both fighters were clearly exhausted when the bell rang.

Confusion again clouded what was clearly a victory for the Minneapolis featherweight. It wasn't until the next day that the victory was finally awarded to Dandy. When the fight ended, the fight's matchmaker, Frank McDonnell, rushed into the ring and held up both fighter's hands to indicate a draw. Dandy was clearly confused and looked to his corner for help. By then, though, the ring was a mass of confusion and the fans began to exit the arena.

McDonnell clearly overstepped his bounds, but the matter wasn't cleared up until the next afternoon when O. F. Wadsworth and F. A. Andretta, the two judges for the fight, announced that they had given the victory to Dandy, as had the referee. The one other judge, Ray Miller, had inexplicably called the fight a draw.

Despite the confusion, Dandy picked up his twentieth victory since turning professional almost three years to the day earlier.

Following his two fights in Montana, Dandy left to join his brother Jack in Los Angeles to begin his "tour" of the West. Jack was fighting exclusively these days on the West Coast and Dandy was anxious to see and experience all that Jack had talked about.

If Hard Work Means Anything, Watch Dandy
* * *   * * *   * * *   * * *
Dillon Is After Title Worn by Tod Morgan

Dandy Dillon of Minneapolis.

NEW RIVALRIES

As Dandy made his way to the West Coast in January of 1923, he was still six months shy of his twenty-first birthday. Dandy, however, was a grizzled veteran of twenty-eight professional prizefights and he had endured 224 rounds of fisticuffs in the three years since he had been fighting. And that didn't count the endless rounds of training in preparation for each of those fights. Dandy didn't realize it, but, even though he was only nineteen-and-a-half years old, it was as if his body had lived a lifetime.

Dandy barely met up with Jack in Los Angeles when Mike Collins told him that he had already lined up his first fight in the L.A. area. Dandy would fight Young Farrell, a veteran West Coast fighter, who had nearly two hundred fights behind him when he stepped into the ring against Dandy.

The first order of business for Dandy was to settle in with Jack who had checked into a downtown hotel. Dandy was anxious to see the Los Angeles area, but Collins wanted to get Dandy into the gym to train for what he expected was to be a tough fight against a hardened veteran.

The match with Farrell was held in Vernon, California, located just five miles south of downtown Los Angeles. Today Vernon is known for its meat-packing plants and slaughterhouses, but in the 1920s, the small town vied with Madison Square Garden as the "Boxing Capital of the World." Legendary promoter Jack Doyle built his outdoor arena in 1908, and it hosted some of the biggest names in the fight game, including Benny Leonard, Mickey Walker, and Jack Dempsey. It was also where you could run into Hollywood celebrities of the day like Charlie Chaplin, "Fatty" Arbuckle, or Mack Sennett's Keystone Kops.

The January 16 bout at the Vernon Avenue Arena was the first time Dandy boxed outdoors. While the evening was cool, the action in the ring was hot. The fight was a preliminary before the scheduled main event between Bud Ridley and Jack Norman, who had substituted for the sick Danny Kramer. Only a scheduled four-rounder, Dandy knew he had the energy to fight fast and hard against the veteran boxer, but Farrell was a smart fighter with plenty of experience.

The match was without a dull moment as both fighters matched punches. Dandy took the first two rounds with his tendency to start fast while Farrell took the final two rounds with the fight ending in a draw.

The fight was more of a tune-up for Dandy as he prepared to fight Tod Morgan the following week at the same venue. Morgan held the Pacific Coast featherweight title, and although only a year older than Dandy, he was a veteran of almost sixty professional fights. This fight was to be the first of three battles between the two featherweights, and would start a rivalry that would last most of the year.

The four-rounder came off without a hitch on January 23, but Dandy found out that Morgan was indeed a championship caliber boxer. Dandy tried to stay with his experienced foe for the four rounds, but found that Morgan's craftiness and speed were simply too much for him. Morgan out-boxed Dandy and eased his way to the decision. Dandy attributed his defeat to simply being tired. Perhaps he was right. This was Dandy's third fight in the span of just fifteen days. After the third loss of his career, Dandy decided he needed a rest.

Jack Josephs was having his own troubles in the Los Angeles area losing twice in the month of January at Hollywood Legion Stadium. Both Dandy and Jack were looking forward to taking a break. Jack was seriously debating whether or not to retire from the ring because of the lack of success he was having, and now it was Danny's turn to lift his older brother's spirits.

They spent the next couple of weeks taking in the sights of Los Angeles, visiting Ocean Park in Santa Monica, seeing Hollywood, and spending time just lying on the beach in Venice. They also took in a few baseball games at Washington Park watching the Los Angeles Angels battle their cross-town rivals, the Vernon Tigers.

February 20 would come too quickly as far as Dandy was concerned. He was enjoying the good life relaxing in the warm Southern California weather, as back home in Minneapolis the temperature was in the low 20s. Johnny Lotsey was his opponent that day, again at the Vernon Avenue Arena.

Dandy didn't get back to the gym until ten days before the scheduled bout, and he really hadn't put his heart back into the training program. Mike Collins tried his best to get Dandy's confidence back up and told him he had scheduled another fight for Dandy in early March against Canadian Bantamweight Champion Vic Foley. This news energized Dandy somewhat, as he relished the idea of holding the Canadian Bantamweight title after securing the Flyweight championship.

Lotsey was no pushover though. He had put together an impressive record of forty-three fights with only eight losses. Lotsey added to that record as Dillon put up another lackluster performance losing the four round decision.

Needless to say, Mike Collins was not happy with Dandy's performance. He told Dandy that this was simply a case of a lack of focus on the task of boxing and not spending enough time in the ring. Dandy didn't disagree with his assessment and vowed to be in better shape by the time they traveled to Seattle for the Vic Foley match.

Dandy had more pressing matters on his mind though. Jack was to be fighting in Hollywood again in three days and Dandy wanted to be there to support his brother who was in his own doldrums.

Dandy attended Jack's fight on February 23, at Hollywood Legion Stadium only to be disappointed as Jack dropped a four-round decision to George Lavigne, whom he had fought a few months earlier to a draw.

The Joseph brothers were reeling, and beginning to second guess their decision to box exclusively on the West Coast. So far, it hadn't been a very friendly experience. If not for the beautiful weather and the luxurious surroundings, they both would have probably packed their bags and headed back home to Minnesota.

Dandy arrived in Seattle several days before his scheduled match but he didn't arrive in the fashion he wanted. He thought it would make for good publicity if he arrived in Seattle by boat, so he arranged transportation to leave from the harbor in San Pedro. The boat had hardly pulled away when Dandy was having second thoughts about his stunt. By the time the boat was three miles away, Dandy was as sick as a dog. When the boat pulled into San Francisco, Dandy made a dash for the railroad office, and used his own money to by a train ticket to Seattle.

Canadian Bantamweight Champion Vic Foley was considered to be one of the finest boxers that Canada had turned out in many years. The British Columbia born fighter learned his boxing trade from his father who ran a boxing gymnasium in Vancouver. The champion was short, standing only five feet three inches tall, three inches shorter than Dillon. However he had yet to be beaten in the ring. In eighteen fights he had walked away with thirteen victories and five draws.

Prior to the March 6 event to be held at Seattle's Crystal Pool, Dandy was working out every afternoon at Austin & Salt's First Avenue Gymnasium and attracting a lot of attention. Dandy and one of the other fighters on the March 6 card, Johnny Mack, staged a three-round workout for the fans in attendance and had the newspapers declaring that "Dillon appears to be in fine shape and ready to give the champion a real busy evening."

Meanwhile, Foley also had been training hard for the bout, which he considered to be the most important of his brief career. Vancouver native Foley was a local fan favorite and was expected to be the favorite going into the ring. Because of Dandy's renown in the east, Foley knew that a victory would enhance his image and give him an opportunity at higher profile fights. He wasn't taking either the fight or Dandy lightly.

The six-round match proved to be a perfectly matched fight from the outset. Dandy started his usual way, bearing down toward the Canadian champion. Foley showed his boxing skills as he fended off the Minnesotan's advances and sidestepped most of Dandy's punches. The first two rounds went to Foley, as Dandy was unable to mount a lasting charge. In the third round, Dandy started to get going and was landing punches with more authority, which had Foley backing up trying to avoid his assaults. The fourth round was much of the same, as Dandy again brought the action toward his foe.

The fight settled down for the final two rounds with both fighters seemingly content that they had done enough in earlier rounds to earn the victory. When the decision was read, referee Ted Whitman raised Foley's arm in victory much to the chagrin of the fans at the Crystal Pool. Judging by the tone of the fans, the vast majority of them were greatly disappointed at the verdict. One newspaper writer thought that, at worst, the decision should have been called a draw. "As we saw it, Vic had the edge in the first two rounds, Dillon a slight lead in the third and fourth with the last two stanzas a standoff. As a result, a draw would have suited the writer better."

Dandy felt that he deserved at least a draw in the bout and was disheartened at suffering his third consecutive loss. He felt he was in great shape and had fought well. He told his manager that it simply took him a little time to figure out Foley's style.

Dandy desperately wanted a rematch with Foley. So did the local writers who thought Dandy deserved better in the first fight. Dandy's fortunes were about to change.

Vic Foley had a match scheduled with Georgie Lee the following Tuesday, but he developed a painful boil on his arm just a couple of days after his bout with Dandy. Foley bowed out of the Lee fight and promoter Dan Salt desperately needed someone to take his place. Dandy, who was still in town, but literally packing his bags to go back to Los Angeles, was contacted by Nate Druxinman, the matchmaker for the fight, and asked to fill in for Foley against Lee. He told Druxinman that he would accept the fight under one condition, which was that if he beat Lee he would get another crack at Foley. Druxinman agreed.

So, when Dandy stepped into the ring just a week later to fight Chinese bantamweight Georgie Lee, he was in excellent shape and had strong motivation to defeat him. Lee, a Sacramento resident, liked to bill himself as the "Chinese bantamweight champion" and promised to be a tough test for Dillon.

Dandy's performance in the first three rounds of the bout was unimpressive and the little jab that Lee kept using was bothering him. The second round was Lee's best, as he repeatedly connected with lefts with few returns by Dandy. A couple of the blows really shook Dandy.

Dandy took command in the fourth round uncorking a vicious attack jarring Lee with a series of rapid-fire rights and lefts. Dandy took the fifth and sixth rounds in similar fashion.

When referee Peter Moe raised Dandy's hand at the end of the fight, the verdict was met with the approval of those in attendance.

Dandy finally had a victory after three losing fights, and he got what he wanted most, a rematch with Vic Foley, and an opportunity to win the Canadian bantamweight championship. He felt truly confident going into the next Foley match.

DANDY DILLON   VIC FOLEY

REMATCH

So far, Dandy's West Coast adventure hadn't been met with the success that he had hoped for. It did, however, introduce him to two of the toughest fighters and competitors he had ever faced. Only the bouts with Frankie Mason equaled the intensity and fervor that came with his fights with Vic Foley and Tod Morgan.

Dandy's fight with Georgie Lee was actually a godsend for Dandy and Mike Collins. First, Lee challenged Dandy and he responded coming back in the fight to win after a lackluster beginning. Second, Dandy badly needed this victory to restore his confidence.

Vic Foley knew his first fight with Dandy was a close one, but he would be going into the second one with first-hand knowledge of how to defend against the Minneapolis boxer, so his confidence was high. The newspapers also thought that while Dandy had a better performance against the "Chinaman," they also said that a Dillon victory "…is possible, but not probable." They considered Dandy fortunate, by way of Foley's inability to fight Lee, to have had three fights within a three-week period and to get the rematch against the bantamweight champion.

The March 20 rematch at the Crystal Palace was something the local fight fans were looking forward to. Many in attendance were also at the first fight two weeks earlier and felt that the fight could have gone either way. They were anxious to see the matter settled.

When the scheduled six-rounder started, it was Foley who was the aggressor. He came out swinging in the first round and caught Dandy a little off guard. Dandy was the one usually starting out fast so this was a change in style. Foley started slower in the first bout and Dandy didn't expect him to change.

The first three rounds found Foley taking most of the initiative. The consensus at ringside was that by the end of the third, Foley was in command of the fight. In the fourth round, Dandy cut loose with a series of punches that landed on the mark and put Foley on the defensive for the first time in the fight. Dandy didn't let up for the balance of the round and continued his aggressiveness into the fifth.

Dandy knew he had to make up ground lost in the first three rounds and never let up for the duration of the fight. As the fight entered the sixth round, Dandy stood toe-to-toe with Foley, exchanging punches with Dandy's doing the most damage. When the match finally ended, Dandy knew it was going to be a close decision.

When the decision was finally read, referee Ted Whitman held Dandy Dillon's hand high, declaring him the winner of the bout and the first conqueror of the Canadian bantamweight champion.

The Northwest and Canadian titles, however, were not relinquished to Dandy. When the weigh-in took place earlier in the evening and the weights were announced as the fighters entered the ring, Dandy weighed in at 126 pounds and Foley weighed 122½ pounds, both too heavy for the bantamweight class. Therefore, the titles could not go to the winner. Although this was the second time a title had escaped Dandy because of weight issues, it didn't bother Dandy that much because he vanquished Foley and had avenged the earlier match, which he strongly believed he hadn't lost. He felt vindicated. In addition, he was the first fighter to hand Foley a defeat.

The following day, Dandy finally packed his bags and caught the train back to Los Angeles. There he reunited with Jack, who was training for an April 3 fight with Ted Krache back in Seattle.

Jack wasn't in the best of spirits when Dandy arrived. He was training daily, but Dandy could tell immediately when he saw Jack in the ring that his heart wasn't in it. In the past eight months, Jack had a total of twelve fights but could only muster a victory in one of them. Jack was telling Dandy that the fight against Krache could be his last.

Dandy did his best to lift his older brother's spirits, but didn't seem to have much effect. He would step into the training ring to spar with him and tell him that he looked good, and that his swing was healthy. Toward the end of Jack's training, Dandy was confident that Jack was starting to feel like his old self again.

Dandy accompanied Jack back to Seattle the following month for his bout with Ted Krache. During the train ride, he cornered Mike Collins and asked him what he thought of Jack's condition. Collins tried to put a positive spin on it, but it was clear to Dandy that he didn't have much confidence in Jack.

Dandy was in Jack's corner the night of his April 3 fight with Ted Krache. Krache brought an impressive 23-2-1 record with thirteen knockouts into the fight against Jack and Dandy feared that Jack might have more than he could handle in the welterweight from Hoquiam, Washington.

Dandy was right. Jack fought gamely for six rounds, but the decision was never in doubt, and Jack lost again for the fifth straight time. Back in the dressing room after the fight, Jack told Dandy that he was done. Dandy could do little to dissuade Jack. Shortly after they got back to Los Angeles, Jack left for Minneapolis to "hang up his gloves."

While Dandy was lamenting Jack's departure, Mike Collins was busy scheduling another bout for his fighter who seemed to regain his form with his two consecutive victories. Before Dandy could settle into his new lifestyle in Los Angeles, Collins had him heading back to Butte, Montana, to face Mike DePinto in a scheduled twelve-round bout.

DePinto, a Portland bantamweight champion in the West, had already had over forty fights coming into the fight on April 17, but it was Dandy who was the crowd favorite. Many remembered his impressive comeback against Ray Rose two years earlier. The bout featured two youngsters with Dandy still shy of his twentieth birthday and DePinto just twenty years old himself. The main event of the Manhattan Athletic Club was held at the Broadway Theater.

The fight opened rather tamely with Dandy poking a few light blows, but he was the aggressor early on. In the second round, Dandy drew first blood by cutting DePinto's lip. DePinto came back in the fourth and fifth rounds to make it a close fight. By the eighth round, Dandy took charge again and in the tenth, both boys landed many times keeping the crowd roaring. In the eleventh, Dandy shot a left to DePinto's jaw, but DePinto countered effectively. At the end of the round, Dillon scored with a series of blows that landed on the mark.

Dandy won the twelve-round decision from DePinto in the same way that he staged his comeback against Rose. Dandy crashed blows to DePinto's body in the twelfth that rocked the Portlander so that all he could do was hang on in the end.

It was an impressive victory for Dandy who was outweighed by his opponent, had a shorter reach, and was shorter in stature. He had also withstood several low blows by DePinto during the bout, but never complained. This caused one newspaper to report, "A cleaner fighter never appeared in the ring in Butte. Minneapolis has sent out many fighters who have proved a credit to the game and Danny is one of them."

Dandy now had three victories in a row and upped his career mark to twenty-three wins, five losses, and six draws. His confidence was up again when he left for Seattle a few days later for his next fight.

In Seattle, Dandy was to face "California" Joe Lynch. Unfortunately for Dandy, it wasn't the same Joe Lynch that he really wanted to fight, the Joe Lynch that was the world champion. Nevertheless, Dandy was looking forward to the fight because of Lynch's reputation.

"California" Joe had beat former bantamweight champion of the world, Johnny Buff, in Buff's first fight after losing the world championship to New York's Joe Lynch. The newspapers felt that Lynch and Dillon were about as evenly matched as they come going into the fight that was held on May 1 at the Arena in Seattle.

Lynch, termed the "human buzz saw" by one local newspaper, came out strong in the first two rounds and took a clear lead over Dandy connecting with body punches that slowed Dandy's usual aggressive start. In the third round, sensing that he had fallen behind considerably in the scheduled six-rounder, Dandy initiated an offensive that caught Lynch off guard and continued for the duration of the round. He renewed his aggressiveness in the fourth and fifth rounds using his right cross effectively and landing the harder punches.

The sixth round was exciting with both fighters somewhat wild, but both anxious to score. Both fighters knew that the outcome of the fight hinged on this round. Lynch scored with body blows, but Dandy was the stronger of the two at the finish.

As the bell rang at the conclusion of the fight, the audience roared their approval. It was clearly a fight that was enjoyed by all. As one reporter put it, "A boxing fan would have to have on an awful grouch to ask for a prettier battle than was staged at the Arena last night between Dandy Dillon, of Minneapolis, and California Joe Lynch in the six-round windup..." When referee Ted Whitman brought both fighters to the center of the ring and raised both their hands, the audience erupted in approval again.

While Dandy certainly wanted a victory in the match, he and Mike Collins both felt that disaster had been averted by Dandy's impressive comeback in the fight.

Next Wednesday's Main Eventers.

Tod Morgan, Promoter Dan Salt, and Dandy Dillon prior to their rematch on September 12, 1923

REMATCH, PART TWO

While in Butte, after the Lynch bout, Mike Collins had other things on his mind. Mike's partner, Mike Gibbons, whose brother Tommy Gibbons was a heavyweight contender at the time, longed for an opportunity to fight Jack Dempsey for the heavyweight crown.

Collins met Loy Molumby, head of Montana's American Legion, in Butte and struck up a friendship with him. When Dandy headed back to Los Angeles, Collins and Molumby traveled around Montana in an old airplane, went target shooting, and drank a lot of wine. During their travels they ended up in Shelby, Montana, and met the Mayor, who was also a local bank manager. Over drinks the three of them talked about fighting and fighters when someone suggested they hold a heavyweight championship fight in Shelby. The mayor felt it would put Shelby on the map and create an overnight land boom.

Before long, Mike was on the phone to his friend and brother's manager, Eddie Kane, with the idea. Kane liked it and told Collins if he could get Dempsey out there Tommy Gibbons would fight him for nothing. Soon afterwards, what was later to be called "Shelby's Folly", the Dempsey-Gibbons fiasco, was born. And Dandy would be part of it!

The Dempsey-Carpentier fight two years earlier produced more than a million dollars at the box office. So, naturally, it was felt by some that staging a Dempsey fight was a gold mine. Body Johnson, the son of the mayor, wired Dempsey's manager, Jack Kearns, an offer of $200,000 to defend his title against the Minnesota heavyweight Tommy Gibbons. Kearns countered with a $300,000 offer. Soon civic pride got in the way of sound business judgment and the local leaders were hammering out the details for a July 4th Dempsey-Gibbons fight.

Three preliminary fights were scheduled for the fight card that day, and with Dandy's manager Mike Collins co-promoting the match, Dandy was paired with Lackey Morrow in a one of them.

When the day of the fight finally arrived, it was painfully clear that the fight was going to be a financial disaster. Only 7,000 spectators paid their way into the outdoor arena. Tommy Gibbons fought for virtually nothing that day but put up a game showing before losing the fight to Dempsey. Business leaders totaled up their losses and four banks eventually failed due to their involvement in the promotion of the fight.

Dandy's fight with Lackey Morrow was cancelled on the day of the fight because of the poor attendance, and the desire of many simply to get the fights over with. Although the business leaders in Shelby were not without fault for the fight's financial failure, most pointed the finger at Dempsey's manager, Jack Kearns, as the real culprit for failing to help promote the fight and for threatening on several occasions, to pull Dempsey out of the bout.

All was not lost for Dandy. During the time he was in Shelby, he trained at the Dempsey camp. There he formed a friendship with Dempsey, with which lasted years after Dandy's boxing career ended.

After the Dempsey-Gibbons fiasco, Dandy headed back to Los Angeles. He had trained hard for his fight with Lackey Morrow and was disappointed that the fight was called off. It also meant that he wouldn't be inside the ring, other than for training, for four months. Dandy was itching to get back in the ring against Tod Morgan.

When Dandy did return to the ring, he found himself, again, traveling to Montana. There, in Butte, he fought Seattle featherweight, Weldon Wing in a twelve-round main event during Butte's Labor Day Celebration.

Weldon "Toughey" Wing had a good reputation as a tough fighter on the West Coast beating many of the same fighters Dandy did such as, Bud Ridley, Mike DePinto, and Sammy Gordon.

On September 2, the match was held under the auspices of the American Legion and Silver Bow Trades and Labor council at Clark Park, an open-air arena. Wing came into the match with many Pacific Coast laurels but ran into a buzz saw when he met Dandy.

The fight was held under two huge arc lights in front of a small crowd bundled up because of the cold weather as they sat in the grandstands and bleachers at ringside. Dandy dominated the majority of the twelve rounds showing Wing his left jab repeatedly while interspersing a right roundhouse when necessary. Wing was no match for Dandy who cruised through the twelve rounds and to his 24th victory. More good news followed his victory when Mike Collins informed Dandy that, in just ten days, he would be fighting that rematch he had hoped for against Tod Morgan in Seattle.

Morgan, the Pacific Coast featherweight champion, had fought seven times since he last met Dandy in January. In six of those fights he arose victorious losing only to Eddie Raimes in a four-round decision. Dandy was on a streak of his own having won four times in his last five bouts with one draw.

When the September 12, match was held at the Arena, Dan Salt and Alonzo Austin expected an entertaining fight. Morgan had established himself in the hearts of the Seattle fans and was a two-to-one favorite going into the bout. Morgan was in superb condition, but was not taking Dandy lightly and told the newspapers he expected a tough fight.

Morgan was coming off of two fights against Bud Ridley where he dominated the fights to retain his Pacific Coast title. Morgan had said that he felt that Ridley's style was such that he simply couldn't match up against him effectively. Morgan said, "Against Dillon I think the fans will find me a more aggressive boy, a fighter more than the boxer I showed against Ridley...Dillon is as aggressive if not more so than Ridley."

However, when the fight began, Morgan started off sluggishly against the typically fast-starting Minnesotan. Dandy easily took the first two rounds carrying the fight to the champion and landing some stirring punches. Morgan took the third round but the fourth was Dandy's by a wide margin. Twice in that round Dandy sent Morgan to the canvas and for a while it looked as if Dandy would finish Morgan off. Morgan's manager, Spider Roach, one newspaper reported, wore a face that "should have been framed and hung in the National Museum of Art."

Between the fifth and the sixth rounds, Roach worked feverishly on the champion and could be seen emphatically talking to him. It wasn't known what was said, but in the final round, Morgan came out "like a Kansas cyclone" and for the next three minutes gave Dandy a boxing clinic. Morgan landed wicked rights and lefts to Dandy's head, which left him dazed. It was a whirlwind comeback for Morgan who used his experience and skill in his effort to bounce back from the obvious lead Dandy had built.

While many of Morgan's supporters in the crowd called for the decision to be given to their favorite, referee Ted Whitman rightfully dubbed the fight a draw. While Morgan clearly won the sixth and final round, Dandy had built up a significant lead going into the final frame and many thought he deserved to win.

It wasn't long after the final bell sounded when Dan Salt was approaching the fighter's managers and asking if they'd like to stage another fight. Both mangers quickly agreed and the stage was set for a third Morgan-Dillon fight to be held in two weeks.

Mike Gibbons and Mike Collins shared managing responsibilities for Dandy Dillon with Gibbons primarily taking care of Dandy's business affairs. The two were convinced that Dandy had the stuff of a champion. When they took over managing Dandy, the two Mikes tried to get Johnny Dundee, then the featherweight champion of the world, to meet him in a championship fight. The fight would have been a ten-round bout held at Fort Snelling, Minnesota. Gibbons and Collins went so far as to get approval from the War Department to stage the title fight. Everything was set in motion for Dandy to have a crack at the world title. However, Dundee had asked for such a prohibitive sum for his services that the match had to be called off.

Gibbons, the former middleweight contender, decided to step up his role in training Dandy for his upcoming Morgan bout. He wanted to show that he still had faith in Dandy's ability to be a world champion. Gibbons took Dandy aside and proceeded to point out his weaknesses, and to brush up his boxing skills.

Going into the September 26 rematch, Dandy thought he had Morgan figured out. When the opening bell rang, Dandy immediately took charge fighting in his usual style with his head down, boring in, and swinging in the clinches. This was Dandy's style, which worked effectively in the past. However, this time it would be Dandy's undoing.

Dillon and Morgan fought evenly in the first round. Then Morgan began to take charge when he won the second round. In the third, the champion started to come into his own and shook Dandy with a hard right. In the fourth round, the two combatants were mixing it up pretty evenly when Dandy again bore in with his head down. Morgan's corner immediately began yelling at the referee, Roy David, arguing that Dandy was using his head. In an instant, to everyone's surprise, David quickly stopped the fight and raised Morgan's hand. Dandy's corner was dumbfounded and Dandy was

DANDY-A Jewish Boxer's Journey

stunned. The referee had disqualified Dandy without so much as a warning.

Pandemonium broke out. *The Seattle Post Intelligencer* reported, "David's action caused a near riot in the ring. Dillon's handlers rushed up to the referee swinging from their hip-pockets, while Morgan's managers and ringside fans hurried to David's defense. Mayor E. J. Brown...dashed through the ropes and waved a threatening finger at the defeated manager and his seconds. The mayor was followed by most of the city police department and order was finally restored."

Customarily referees warned a boxer before disqualifying him. So, many thought that it was strange that David did not stop the fight and give Dillon a warning. After the fight, *The Boxing Blade*, opined that the local boxing commission had been having difficulty in securing qualified referees for bouts. Consequently, David was probably unaware that a warning usually precedes disqualification. Therefore, his action in raising Morgan's arm so suddenly caused much surprise, although the local fans met the move with general support.

Dandy was devastated by the decision. He felt that he had the clear lead going into that fourth round and was confident that he would hold off the champion for the final two rounds. To compound his misery, he was fined $100 for head butting, which he had to pay to a community fund. He would never know if he could have beaten Morgan. That was the last time the two would fight.

Morgan would go on to a long career, fighting until 1942, when he was nearly forty years old. He won more than 130 fights over a career that found him in the ring over 200 times. He served in the Australian army in World War II before returning to the United States to work as a referee.

Dandy wasted no time leaving Seattle vowing never to return to that Pacific Northwest city. He caught the train back to Los

Angeles the next day and pondered his future on the train ride back.

Dandy "boxing" with Burlesque Dancer and
Actress Sally Rand (Billy Beck)

HOLLYWOOD

On the ride down to Los Angeles, he wrote Jack a letter asking how he was doing. However, he primarily wanted to commiserate with him about the results of the Morgan fight. When he got back to Los Angeles, he also took time to write letters to other friends. He was feeling alone in the city without Jack there and a letter from home was always welcome.

One of the letters he wrote was to his friend Ernie Fliegel. Fliegel was another Minneapolis boxer who Dandy befriended at the local gym. Fliegel was a lightweight who met with moderate success, and had his career cut short when he lost an eye in the ring in 1927. Like Dandy, he was a Jewish immigrant coming to America from Romania in 1910. After leaving the ring, he tried his hand at managing fighters but eventually opened a restaurant with his partner Max Winter (who would eventually found the Minnesota Vikings football team) in 1935. He later was a silent partner with Winter when he helped form the Minneapolis Lakers in the late 1940s.

Both Jack and Ernie wrote Dandy back with words of encouragement. Jack was trying to establish himself in business opening up a delicatessen. Yet he was concerned about Danny's well being. Jack knew what it was like to be disappointed in the ring, so he tried his best to tell Danny to forget about the past and concentrate on the future.

That future was to be without the guidance of Mike Collins and Mike Gibbons. Dandy had told them, after the last Morgan bout, that it was his intention to fight primarily in Southern California. He liked the area and had grown weary of the travel. Collins and Gibbons wanted him to fight more in the Midwest closer to their Minnesota home. As a result, the pair parted company with Dandy, but wished him well nonetheless. They referred him to a local fight manager, Willie "Gig" Rooney, who agreed to make Dandy part of his stable of fighters.

Dandy decided the best cure for his blues was to fight his way out of it. It was a little over a month before Dandy stepped back into the ring. When he did, it was against New Yorker Frankie Brown in Hollywood.

Brown was a journeyman boxer who was trying to extend his career by moving to the West Coast. He didn't have any success against Dandy. The four-rounder on November 2, at the Legion Stadium wasn't much of a contest. While he didn't knock Brown out, Dandy did everything short of it by winning the decision.

Rooney scheduled Dandy's next fight a month later in Stockton, California. There he was to meet native Californian Joe Bell in the main event at the Poppy Bowl on December 7.

Bell, from Pittsburg, did not enjoy the same reputation as Dandy. Dandy was making his debut in Stockton, but was well known for his bouts on the West Coast. Boxing promoters "Buck" Holley and Roger Cornell were already promising local fans that if Dillon got by Bell they would match him with "Dynamite" Joe Murphy, another promising California boxer. Bell outweighed Dandy by a few pounds and the promoters thought that might even things out for Bell who lacked Dandy's skills in the ring.

Dandy's fight with Bell didn't even last five minutes. In the first round, Bell came out strong and landed three solid blows to Dandy midsection backing him into a corner. Suddenly, Dandy responded, and landed a vicious blow to Bell's head sending him reeling backwards. Bell started to recover, but eventually fell. Bell got up and came back at Dandy as fiercely as he had at the outset but was met again by a hard right to the stomach by Dandy that floored the Californian and sent him down for a nine-count. Bell came back but was staggered twice more before the bell rang.

Bell seemed refreshed by the break between rounds and came out strong again for the second. He fought gamely for about a minute before Dandy caught him with a right cross that sent him back to the canvass. Before he could get up, his corner had tossed in the towel ending the fight.

Dandy was extremely pleased with his performance, and who wouldn't be? He scored his eighth knockout while picking up his twenty-sixth victory. His record was an impressive 26-6-8. By virtue of this victory over Bell, Dandy was now scheduled to fight "Dynamite" Murphy the following week.

Dandy had impressed the Stockton fans so much with his quick work of Joe Bell that they were looking forward to the bout at the Poppy Bowl with Murphy. Murphy had a reputation as a hard-hitter, so the fans felt that a Dillon-Murphy match would be a wild one.

The December 14 main event was garnering a lot of activity. Advanced sales for the bout far outpaced the sales for the previous two weeks at the Poppy.

The fight fans weren't disappointed. Dandy floored Murphy with a right to the face in the first round of the scheduled four-rounder. Murphy had the count go to nine before he was able to scrape himself off the floor to resume the fight. From that point on, Dandy had a commanding lead and continued to take the fight to Murphy for the duration.

Dandy had no serious trouble keeping ahead of his adversary and Murphy could score no more than a few punches in the third round. The fourth round was all Dandy's as he punished Murphy repeatedly with his left. Dandy clearly dominated the entire fight to win the decision. John J. Peri, a writer for a local newspaper reported, "They will have to trot out better boys than "Dynamite" Murphy of Sacramento if they expect to beat "Dandy" Dillon in this town."

Back in Los Angeles, Dandy enjoyed the weather, the atmosphere, and on many occasions, the limelight. Performing in Los Angeles, especially Hollywood, had its perks and its distractions.

It was not uncommon at the Hollywood Legion Stadium to find movie actors and other celebrities taking in a fight and rubbing elbows with some of the boxers. People like Charlie Chaplin, Fatty Arbuckle, Lon Chaney, Boris Karloff, Mae West, Al Jolson, and the Marx Brothers as well as the likes of Ernest Hemingway, could be found in the arena enjoying the festivities.

Hollywood Legion Stadium was one of three major boxing venues in the Los Angeles area that saw its share of celebrity viewers. Along with the Arena in Vernon and the Wilmington Bowl, Hollywood Legion Stadium hosted regular Friday night fights. It began as an open arena in 1921 and soon added an arc roof to accommodate 5,000 spectators. Later, the Olympic Auditorium would open and become the premiere boxing venue in Southern California.

—Illustrated Daily News Photo.

MAY CARRY A MESSAGE TO GARCIA—That is, via his fists, for Dandy Dillon, the Minneapolis featherweight, will take on Frankie Garcia in the main event tonight at the Hollywood American Legion boxing stadium.

THE TURNING OF THE TIDE

After the "Dynamite" Murphy bout, Dandy upped his record to twenty-seven wins and eight draws with only six losses, two of which he avenged. But Dandy was going to hit a stretch in the days and months ahead that would test him physically and emotionally. Dandy was used to being a winner and a champion. Although he was only twenty years old as 1924 approached, Dandy was a veteran of forty-one professional prizefights and had boxed in the ring a total of 310 rounds.

Dandy traveled to Oakland for his next bout, which was to be part of a New Year's extravaganza at the Oakland Auditorium. His January 1, 1924, match was with Joe Leopold for the four-rounder. He hadn't trained much for the fight and because he had beaten "Dynamite" Murphy so easily a little more than two weeks earlier, he entered the bout with much confidence. That confidence, however didn't equate to a victory.

Dandy carried the match to Leopold from the outset and did so in each round of the tilt against the popular Oakland fighter. But the judges didn't see it that way and gave Leopold the verdict ignoring Dandy's aggressiveness throughout the bout. He weakened somewhat in the fourth, but most there felt the worst he should have received was a draw. Dandy wasn't as bothered by the decision as one might expect. He felt that he had boxed well enough to earn a victory and shook it off as a hometown decision.

Dandy was anxious to get back to Los Angeles and left the next day on the morning train. Willie Rooney had already scheduled his next bout for January 11, against a tough eastern opponent, Frankie Garcia.

Garcia had already made a name for himself on the West Coast before heading south to fight successfully in Georgia, Tennessee, Illinois, and Nebraska. He first gained fame winning the Pacific Coast amateur bantamweight title fighting for the Los Angeles Athletic Club at San Francisco. From there he parlayed a successful string of victories in Southern California before turning eastward. However, this was Garcia's first bout in Los Angeles fighting mostly at the Vernon Arena when in Southern California

Garcia was bringing a string of six consecutive victories into the bout with Dandy, entering the fight as the favorite. Garcia had been fighting since 1916, when he won his first fight at the Vernon Arena fighting under the moniker, "The Masked Marvel."

The fight at Hollywood Legion Stadium started in a typical Dandy fashion. Dandy did all the leading throughout the fight while Garcia seemed contented countering Dandy's punches. Dandy piled up points in the first and second rounds against the flashy Garcia. The packed house was enjoying the fisticuffs in the fourth round when Garcia caught Dandy with several stinging rights.

When the verdict was read, Garcia was declared the victor, but many thought Dandy deserved better. Reporter Billy Van felt that while Garcia had been a big sensation in the South, "the wise old birds went out muttering to themselves that there must be an awful poor crop of feathers in the South and East or else Garcia was being given more than his share of press notices, for he had his hands full in defeating "Dandy" Dillon tonight; in fact, many thought Dillon should have had his hand raised for making it a fight."

Garcia was a defensive fighter and this time Dandy's aggressiveness probably cost him the match. Garcia simply waited until Dandy left himself open and made the best of those opportunities. Garcia didn't score many punches, but when he did, they were effective. This was a case where being flashy was more important that landing the most punches.

Other reporters felt that Dandy deserved a rematch because they felt the decision wasn't just and called for matchmaker Tom Kennedy to give Dillon another shot at Garcia because he deserved it. Dandy eventually would get that rematch, but it didn't come soon enough. He would have to wait nearly two years to get it.

Shortly after the Garcia fight, Dandy received a letter from Jack in Minneapolis. He had decided to resume his boxing career back in Minnesota. Jack's comeback was met with mixed results. He would fight another five times winning twice and losing once with two no decisions. He would finally hang up the gloves for good after a ten-round defeat at the hands of Johnny Tillman on June 24, 1924, in Minneapolis.

Dandy, meanwhile, was fuming over the Garcia decision. Once again, he felt he was robbed of victory and was starting to become cynical of the game.

His next fight was in February against Larry Murphy, who was "Dynamite" Murphy's brother. In his previous thirteen fights, Murphy only came away a victor once. "Gig" Rooney was worried about his little firebrand after his loss to Garcia. Dandy's manager felt Dandy didn't have the same fire in him that he was used to seeing and it was evident again in the Murphy fight.

Larry Murphy was a journeyman who, under normal conditions, Dandy would have torn apart in their four-round match. Instead, all Dandy could muster against Murphy was a draw. Dandy had closed Murphy's left eye, bloodied his nose, and sent him to the canvas once, but was unable to put him away. And for the first time, Dandy himself was caught off guard and knocked down for the first time in his career. Once again, Dandy felt he deserved better.

Emotionally, Dandy was a battered man. He felt he simply couldn't catch a break, and was becoming disenchanted with boxing in general. If it wasn't for the purses, Dandy might have followed Jack into retirement. But as a twenty year old, Dandy didn't know any other trade. As far as he was concerned, boxing was his calling.

"Gig" Rooney tried his best to tell Dandy he was the better fighter in his last two matches and that he shouldn't let the judge's decisions bother him. He told him that the best way to prove them wrong was to get back into the ring and show them.

Dandy climbed back into the ring at Hollywood Legion Stadium on February 22, against "Cowboy" Eddie Anderson. Anderson, originally from Chicago but calling Wyoming home, was a workhorse who would go on to have over 250 bouts in his career.

The fight started even in the first round, but the hard-hitting Anderson scored in the second, landing a hard right hand that shook Dandy. Dandy came alive in the third round and easily outboxed Anderson. In the fourth, Dandy tried to go for the win, but Anderson's right hand was too effective and one blow sent Dandy to one knee. He got up immediately and finished the round aggressively, but when all was said and done, Anderson was given the verdict.

This time Dandy knew he was on the short end. He simply lost the fight. Anderson was too hard a hitter to go toe-to-toe with, and Dandy knew he should have fought more defensively. There was no question in his mind that he was the better boxer, but he knew he couldn't punch harder than Anderson.

Ten days later, Dandy found himself in a rematch with Larry Murphy. This outcome was worse than the first fight. He lost the four-round decision to Murphy at the Arena in Vernon on March 4. The *Los Angeles Times* reported that, "Dandy started in like Jack Dempsey and had the opener but after that Larry led the march."

Dandy kept it close in the second but Murphy took charge in the third and almost put Dandy through the ropes in the fourth.

After his fifth fight in succession without a victory, Dandy told "Gig" Rooney that he'd had enough. Rooney tried to convince him it was something all boxers went through and to hang in there. He encouraged Dandy to take some time off and regroup.

For the next two months, Dandy did a lot of soul searching. He wondered if he should follow Jack's lead and simply give up the ring. But he would tell himself that he was young. After all, he was still only twenty years old, and he still had a lot of fight left in him. In early April, he called Rooney and told him that he wanted back in the ring.

Rooney thought that a change of scenery might be what Dandy needed and scheduled him for a ten-round bout in Vancouver, Canada, against Len Malody on April 25. Malody was a hard hitter from Laramie, Wyoming, who called himself "The Lonesome Timberwolf."

Malody hadn't lost in his previous five outings coming into the fight at the Brighouse Arena. With Dandy coming in with a mirror image of Malody's last five fights, he didn't carry a lot of confidence with him. Dandy held his own throughout the bout, but never managed to get anything going. The fight went the distance and ended in a draw.

Dandy stayed in the Pacific Northwest another week to fight Bud Ridley in Tacoma, Washington, on May 1. Ridley was a fellow Minnesotan and was coming back after suffering a broken arm in a fight the previous September. He had hit his opponent so hard in the forehead that he broke two bones in his right forearm. His fight with Dandy was only his second fight since he returned to the ring, the first fight having resulted in a victory. Ridley was a veteran fighter who once held the Pacific Coast featherweight title and had been fighting five years longer than Dandy.

The fight was held at the Kay Street Athletic Club for the benefit card to support the children's Wild West Camp of the Veterans of Foreign Wars. When Dandy entered the ring, it was apparent from the start that he was simply going through the motions. He entered the ring at 130 pounds which was the heaviest weight he fought at. He was not in shape. Ridley easily won the six-round decision and Dandy again went into "semi-retirement."

Dandy pondered his fate in Los Angeles hardly stepping into the training ring for over three months. When he finally decided to lace them up again, he travelled half way across the country to fight Ray Miller in Aurora, Illinois. Miller, a Chicagoan, was an eighteen-year-old upstart who packed a prolific knockout punch. He entered the fight with Dandy with an 18-1 record with thirteen of those victories, including the one just prior to the bout with Dandy, coming by way of the knockout. It was really unclear why Dandy's manager scheduled the fight with such a comer when Dandy was on an obvious downturn.

The results of the fight were predictable and on August 11, 1924, Dandy suffered the biggest indignity he had ever suffered in the ring. He was knocked out in the second round by Miller. While he started the fight in good fashion, *The Los Angeles Times* reported, "…he was knocked colder that a newly-risen spring."

After the fight, Dandy again told "Gig" Rooney that he just didn't have it any more. Rooney told Dandy that he should go home to Minneapolis and consider what he really wanted to do, as being around family would be the best thing for him. So Dandy did exactly that and left straight from Aurora to Minneapolis on the first train out the next morning.

In Minneapolis, he was reunited with the people he cared about most in the world, his family. He spent time with his parents, brothers and sisters, as well as his friends. Within a couple of days, Dandy was happier than he'd been in months. While everyone was encouraging Dandy, the mere fact that he was home again made all the difference in the world.

Dandy's father, Nathan, sat down with him and told him that the most important decision that he could make was one that he and he alone made. Nathan reasoned with Danny that it was how he felt about himself that was important, and not what others thought about him.

Jack's words also were uplifting to Danny. Jack told Danny that he was doing well and was happy; although he missed the ring, he also realized he didn't have the same skills anymore and got tired of being a punching bag. Jack told Danny that whatever decision he made, he would support him.

Dandy loved boxing and wanted more than anything to continue his career. So after spending two weeks in Minneapolis, Dandy limped back home to Los Angeles and attempted to lift his bruised spirit. He stayed away from the gym completely and simply tried to enjoy life. He had saved much of his earnings from the ring, but he still didn't know what he would do. He was twenty-one now, but wasn't sure how he would be able to earn a living outside of the boxing ring.

After not putting on the gloves for several weeks, he finally returned to the gym determined to regain his form and his winning ways inside the ropes. In his heart, Dandy knew he would continue to fight even though his heart was not completely in it. At this point in his career, he was fighting to make a living. But he honestly felt that, at age twenty-one, he was still in his prime as a boxer. But, his body had taken a lot of punishment in the past five years and while he wouldn't admit it to himself, his skills were declining.

Dandy in Los Angeles 1925

A ROLLER COASTER RIDE

"Gig" Rooney sat down with Dandy in mid-September and asked him what he wanted to do. Dandy told him that he wanted to fight and asked him to get him a match. Dandy seemed determined to prove to himself and to Rooney that he still had some sock left in him.

Rooney obliged and arranged a fight for him at the Wilmington Bowl with a local boy named Billy Hogan on October 8. Hogan had been making a stir locally by going undefeated in his first five fights.

Dandy had renewed vigor coming into the fight and had been training hard for the last few weeks. When the bell rang at the start of the first round, it was the Dandy of old. He came in typical style with his head down and boring forward and for four rounds he gave the young upstart from Long Beach a boxing lesson. In the second round, he brought the crowd to their feet when he sent Hogan down for a count of nine. Hogan was hurt, but came back up swinging and finished the round. In the third, Dandy sent him to the canvas once more, but he bounced up again. Dandy finished the fourth in fine form and easily won the decision. Dandy's only disappointment with the fight was that he couldn't put Hogan down for the count. However, he was impressed with the youngster's determination.

Dandy was happy once more. The visit home to Minnesota lifted his spirits, but a victory in the ring was even more uplifting. He was anxious to fight again and soon. So Rooney obliged and arranged for him to fight Benny Dotson at the Wilmington Bowl on October 22.

Dotson had been around for a couple of years and had an impressive record. He'd fought both Bud Ridley and Tod Morgan to draws and had lost only three times in his eighteen fights. While Dotson, from Portland, was a better than average boxer, he wasn't a hard puncher. The Wilmington Athletic Club had the Dillon v. Dotson match as their main event. Dandy was always a crowd pleaser and a large draw.

The fight was entertaining for the fans. It was clear from the start that Dandy was the superior boxer. Dandy had built up what appeared to be an insurmountable lead when the third round started. Dotson came to life and was able to land enough punches that the four-rounder ended in a draw.

Dandy wasn't disappointed at the result; he was simply frustrated that he wasn't able to finish the job. However, the promoters and the fans were thoroughly entertained and quickly scheduled a rematch for the following week. That fight ended with the same result. In a virtual replay of the first match, the November 5, bout ended in the same fashion, another draw for Dandy.

While Dandy wasn't pleased that he didn't get the victories against Dotson, he was beginning to feel like his old self. He fought well and thought that if it were not for Dotson's propensity to clinch, that he would have gotten in more solid shots. Then he would have earned the win. But, Dandy was encouraged that he had gone three fights without losing and was growing in confidence when he entered the ring against Richie King two weeks later.

"Sailor" Richie King was the All-Navy featherweight champion and an experienced fighter. He was stationed on the U.S.S. Maryland, which was conveniently moored in Long Beach at the time of the bout when he fought Dandy at the Wilmington Bowl on November 19.

The fight was full of action from the outset as Dillon and King battled in whirlwind fashion. But neither one of them was able to gain the upper hand nor damage the other fighter by the time the four-round fight concluded. The fight was declared a draw to the delight of the packed house.

Dandy had fought four times in the last month and a half. Now he decided it was time for a break. He was pleased with the progress he was making and wanted to rest up before starting the new year. After taking the rest of the year off, Dandy went back to training in January, 1925.

He met journeyman Gene Delmont at Hollywood Legion Stadium on February 6. Delmont had over 80 bouts entering the fight and had been fighting since Dandy first came to the shores of America from Grigoriopol as an eight-year old boy. He was also a prolific loser having lost over fifty of those matches.

But even with all of Delmont's history, Dandy was unable to put him away in their match. In fact, after scuffling for six rounds, the referee raised Delmont's hand in victory much to Dandy's chagrin. Dandy knew he hadn't fought well, but he didn't think he lost. Losing to Delmont didn't do much for Dandy's confidence.

As frustrated as he was with the Delmont bout, Dandy wanted to get back in the ring quickly. He did just that a week later back in Wilmington against Pico Ramies on February 11.

Raimes was a local boy who resided in Wilmington and brought an impressive 16-6-4 record into the bout. Although he had lost his previous three fights, Raimes was considered a tough opponent who wanted badly to get by Dandy to pad his resume and secure some more profitable fights.

Coming off his loss to Delmont, Dandy was determined to get back on the winning track. He did just that. Dandy won the eight round match fairly easily. He scored points from the outset and chased Raimes for much of the bout. It was an easy call for the judges and Dandy returned to the winner's circle with the decision.

The Wilmington crowd was pleased as usual with the results and especially with Dandy. He had gained a large following in the southland with his aggressive style and the fans clamored for more. The Wilmington Athletic Club listened and Dandy was set for a rematch with Richie King two weeks later on February 25.

The Dillon v. King main event at the Wilmington Bowl was one of three bouts that night that featured fighters from the Navy fleet. Besides "Sailor" Richie, the fight card that night saw "Sailor" Mike Hector facing Duke Potter in the semi-windup and in an all Navy match "Sailor" Don Levy met "Sailor" Paddy Mullen.

The second Dillon v. King fight was another close one. Both fighters were on their toes throughout the ten-round bout and the fight could have gone either way. In the fifth round, Dandy landed a hard right to King's head, which shook Dandy's hand so much he was unable to use it with any effectiveness for the rest of the fight. As a consequence, King was handed the decision and Dandy left the ring again shaking his head with disappointment and in disbelief. He knew the fight was close and felt he had earned no worse than a draw. He was angry that, with his injured hand, he wasn't able to punch his way to a win.

The fight promoters were so pleased with the Dillon-King matchups that they wanted a third fight for March 25. However, by the time the date rolled around, Dandy's hand still hadn't recovered fully. He had to pull out of the match.

The past year had been such a roller coaster ride for Dandy. So with his hand still hurting, Dandy decided to take another hiatus from the ring. He headed back to Minneapolis for some rest and relaxation.

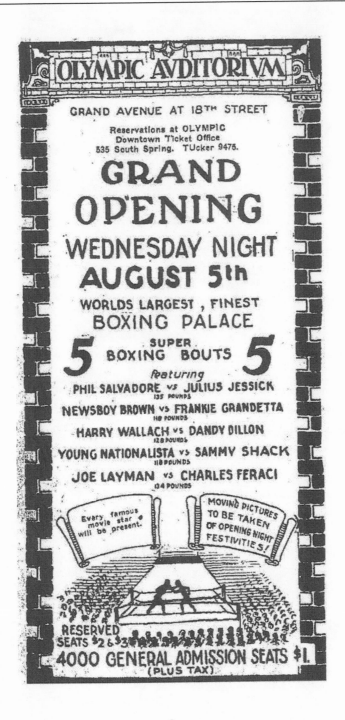

THE CLOSING ROUND

Dandy spent three months at home in Minneapolis. He enjoyed spending time with his family and attending some local boxing matches with his brothers Jack, Sam, and Dave. He especially enjoyed watching his good friend Ernie Fliegel defeat Nick Oliva on March 27 in St. Paul. Ernie was just starting his career and now had two consecutive wins over the fellow St. Paul native.

Dandy returned to Los Angeles in mid-June. He started training diligently at "Gig" Rooney's Newsboy's Gym in preparation for his next fight, which was to be held at a new boxing arena called the Olympic Auditorium.

From 1901 through 1904, Hazard's Pavillon in Los Angeles was the toast of the West Coast boxing venues. It hosted prizefights, which included two future heavyweight champions of the world, Jim Jeffries and Jack Johnson. Hollywood Legion Stadium, Vernon Arena, and the Wilmington Bowl filled the void after that. But it was not until the Olympic Auditorium opened in 1925 that Los Angeles truly had a world-class arena for boxing.

Construction on the $1,000,000 arena began in 1924 with Jack Dempsey turning the ceremonial first shovel of dirt and was built specifically to host wrestling, weightlifting, and boxing events for the 1932 Los Angeles Olympics. In its later life, it would be the setting for Hollywood movies *The Champ*, *Rocky*, and *Million Dollar Baby*.

Olympic Auditorium Manager, Jack Root, was anxious to have opening night on August 5, 1925, be an event to be remembered. The Olympic would be the largest boxing arena in the world seating 15,000 spectators and one which *Los Angeles Times* reporter Paul Lowry called a "...great concrete mansion of maul." Root put together a strong card with lightweights Phil Salvadore and Julius Jessick billed as the main event.

Also on the card that night, Dandy Dillon was scheduled to meet Harry Wallach, which many thought would be the more interesting fight. Wallach was a southpaw who had earlier defeated Jackie Fields in the Olympic trials and Dandy was a crowd favorite who always generated large crowds.

All six bouts were scheduled as six-round events and the Olympic was sold out by the time the fights began at 8:30 p.m. Many boxing and Hollywood celebrities were in attendance including Jack Dempsey, James L. Jeffries, and Rudolph Valentino. Phil Salvadore won the main event that night from Julius Jessick (to a chorus of boos from the crowd!) but Dandy was unable to make the opening bell. Earlier in the day, Dandy came down with a terrible stomach bug and Dave Machado had to substitute for him. Wallach decisioned Machado in the six-rounder.

Disappointed that he was unable to make the start, he was at Rooney's gym a few days later back in training. Rooney had secured a rematch with a fighter Dandy had been itching to fight again over a year and a half ago, Frankie Garcia.

Hollywood Legion Stadium was host for the September 16 main event rematch with Garcia. Garcia was being touted as a contender for the world championship, as he had recently defeated Bud Ridley and Gene Delmont. However, he was coming off of a defeat two months earlier to Jimmy Hackley. Still, he brought over thirty victories into his match with Dandy.

The twenty-two-year old Dandy fought gamely against Garcia, but he was unable to put anything together against the future member of the World Boxing Hall of Fame. Dandy lost the six-round decision.

It was another month before his next prizefight, which was held in Fresno at the Civic Auditorium against Kid Kopecks. Kopecks was a coming fighter and not afraid to mix it up with anybody. The ten-round bout was put on by the American Legion on October 13, and was another in which Dandy showed little or no flash. He fought gamely for the ten rounds, but never had a solid round against Kopecks and lost the decision.

Dandy once again was having thoughts of hanging up the gloves. He wasn't winning with any consistency. In fact the opposite was true. But, he had the periodic win or draw to keep him going. His next fight, though, wouldn't be until April 6, 1926, and he had to travel to Portland, Oregon, for that fight.

Leading up to that fight, Dandy suffered another embarrassing indignity. On the night of December 30, 1925, Dandy went to the Olympic Auditorium to watch the boxing card. After the last match, Dandy was leaving the auditorium with the crowd. In the hustle of the crowd, a man had his pocket picked. The man began yelling. Rex Laws, a fire commissioner, was standing nearby and thought he saw Dandy hand something to another person, believing it to be the man's wallet. Laws detained Dandy until a police officer was called and Dandy was arrested. Dandy spent seventy-two hours in jail before the charges were dismissed prompting *Los Angeles Times* reporter Paul Lowry to write in his column, Rabbit Punches:

> "Little Dandy Dillon spent seventy-two hours in jail last week because somebody made a big mistake. The featherweight boxer was heaved into the city bastile on complaint of a man who had his pocket picked in front of the Olympic Auditorium. Later it developed that the man was utterly wrong, and Dandy was released—with

apologies. Apologies are nice, but they don't altogether take away the sting of an unjust accusation. Investigation at the time might have saved Dandy considerable mortification."

Dandy wasn't thrilled about going back to the Pacific Northwest, but Rooney had scheduled a fight against Len Malody, with whom he fought a ten-round draw in Vancouver, British Columbia, two years earlier. The Pacific Northwest wouldn't be kind to Dandy this time either.

Dandy's last few fights had been as a lightweight and it was apparent that it wasn't an ideal weight to fight at for a couple of reasons. First, he was not used to carrying the extra weight, and second, it usually meant that his opponents were stronger fighters than the ones he had been used to fighting.

The main event at the Armory didn't last long. As reported by the *Portland Oregonian*, "one minute and 48 seconds after the lightweight main event at the Armory last night started, Len Malody of Laramie, Wyo., crashed a murderous right to the jaw of Dandy Dillon of Minneapolis. Dillon fell on his face, tried to get up at the count of seven and then fell forward again, unconscious. His seconds worked on the stricken fighter several minutes before he came to."

That was the final straw for Dandy. He felt humiliated and in the dressing room that evening he told "Gig" Rooney that he would never fight again.

He took the train back to Los Angeles two days after the fight and then promptly packed his clothes and caught the next train back to Minneapolis.

For the next year, Dandy pondered what he would do next in life. He still loved the game of boxing and he relished the thrill of being in the ring. Instead of finding work in Minneapolis, he found himself at the local gym helping out other young fighters and occasionally putting on the gloves to spar.

While he did go to boxing matches in the area catching as many of his friend, Ernie Fliegel's matches as he could, most of his time was spent with his family. He talked to Jack a lot and told him how much he missed being in the ring. Jack had gone through a similar experience when he quit the ring. He even eventually went back for a few bouts before he hung up his gloves for good. Jack wondered aloud if Dandy ought to do the same. He told Dandy that if he still had the itch, and didn't follow up on it, he might never forgive himself.

Dandy finally made the decision to give it one more try. He phoned "Gig" Rooney in Los Angeles and told him to arrange a match for him. Rooney consented and arranged for Dandy to meet Tony Cruz in El Rio for his comeback.

El Rio was north of Los Angeles and east of Oxnard. Dandy wanted to ease back into the ring before returning directly to the Los Angeles area. The eight-round bout was the featured fight on the American Legion card but the young Mexican challenger would prove to be no test for Dandy. Cruz had only three wins in twenty-seven previous fights but Dandy felt he needed an easy win in the first fight of his comeback.

Dandy had the better of Cruz for the first five rounds, but was unable to put him away. Cruz had strong rounds in the sixth and seventh and easily won those two. But Dandy came on strong in the final stanza to win the referee's decision.

With the first victory of his comeback secure, Dandy wanted someone more challenging for his next bout. He found that challenge in Pico Raimes whom he had defeated over two years earlier. The May 25 fight marked Dandy's return to the Wilmington Bowl.

The scheduled eight-rounder would only go six rounds. Raimes pounded Dandy at will throughout the fight and the referee finally stopped the bout in the sixth round for a TKO. A couple months shy of his twenty-fourth birthday, Dandy's boxing career was over.

For seven and a half years, Dandy Dillon toiled in the boxing ring ending with a record of 30 wins, 18 losses, and 13 draws in 61 professional prizefights. He toiled in the ring for 423 rounds of boxing. He had 8 knockouts. Dandy began his career with a brilliant 27-6-8 record. However, the past two years had been brutal. He had twenty fights in the past 30 months and was only able to win three of those while securing five draws.

But Dandy was a champion! The little Jewish immigrant from Russia had held the featherweight championship of Canada; he had defeated the bantamweight champion of Canada; he had defeated the American featherweight champion; he had defeated the Scottish flyweight champion. No one would ever be able to take those accomplishments away from the diminutive lad. He was indeed, a Dandy!

*Dandy and His Parents, Eva and Nathan Joseph,
circa 1935*

EPILOGUE

Before he reached his twenty-fourth birthday, Moishe Josofsky, a Jewish immigrant, had escaped the pogroms of Czarist Russia, made his mark in the streets of Minneapolis selling newspapers, became a professional boxer, and achieved championship stardom. But what was a twenty-three-year-old washed up pugilist to do for the rest of his life?

After Dandy's last bout, he didn't entirely leave the boxing world. For several years he continued as a sparring partner for his former manager "Gig" Rooney. Later, he and Rooney became partners managing fighters. In 1929, he sparred with Ace Hudkins who was training to meet Mickey Walker for the world middleweight championship. (Hudkins would lose that bout to Walker in a ten-round decision.) When Kay Owe wrote about Hudkins' training for the fight in the *Los Angeles Times,* she mentioned that Hudkins "...worked with Dandy Dillon, an old-timer from the four-round days." "Old-timer" Dandy was only twenty-six years old!

In the early 1930's, many "washed up" fighters settled in Southern California, especially in the Los Angeles area, when their fighting days were done. Many didn't have much to show for the time they toiled in the ring and they sought to begin anew in another line of business. Movie lots abounded with old-timers trying to land bit parts in film, but most made livings in an ordinary fashion. They became bell hops, electricians, realtors, lawyers, and the like.

Danny opened up his own beer garden in Los Angeles, but still kept his hand in the boxing game. He and Rooney managed "Silent" Joe Hill, a deaf-mute heavyweight sensation who, in 1938, started his career after winning the Pacific Golden Gloves Heavyweight Title by winning his first four fights and seven of his first nine bouts. However, "Silent" Joe never lived up to his early promise and only won one more fight out of his next twenty before calling it a career.

But Danny did well with his beer garden. He regaled patrons by shadow boxing and telling stories about the "old" days in the ring, and occasionally using his boxing skills to provide "security" in his place of business. *Los Angeles Times* columnist, Bill Potts wrote in 1935, that "Danny Dillon is tougher than he was when in the ring. He exercises an hour every morning to stay in shape to keep order in his beer palace...Don't say we didn't warn you."

In late 1938, Danny would suffer the greatest loss of his life. His brother Jack had been suffering severe headaches most likely as a result of the many blows he absorbed during his years in the ring. On the evening of December 12, 1938, Danny called Jack to wish him a happy birthday. The conversation didn't last very long. Jack was crying in agony over the severe pain in his head. Danny knew that Jack's headaches were becoming progressively more painful, but didn't realize the severity of them. Jack told Danny he simply couldn't take it anymore. While on the phone with his beloved brother, Danny heard a shot. Jack had taken his own life.

That event traumatized Danny, and while he eventually recovered from the initial shock, he never really got over the loss of his brother. As a result he developed a strong hatred for guns, and long before it became a political debate, Danny was a strong advocate for gun control.

Danny later moved to San Francisco to open up a restaurant and cocktail lounge with his old friend, Harry Pelsinger. Harry was a successful former boxer in his own right with thirty-eight ring victories. These Jewish friends opened the Club Continental at 127 Ellis Street in San Francisco in the early 1940s.

After the war broke out in 1941, Danny, very patriotic as a naturalized citizen, wanted to do something for his country. But at the age of thirty-eight, military service was not a realistic option. He had read about the treatment of Jews in Germany and wanted desperately to do his part for the war effort, so he joined the Merchant Marines. He didn't serve long, but it was his way of participating.

Danny had married twice before he and Harry opened the restaurant, but those marriages to Fay and Helen were short-lived. In 1942 he had hired a young singer to perform at his club and he was immediately smitten with the twenty-one year old Adelyne. Adelyne performed nightly at the Club Continental and her radio show on radio station KYA, "Songs by Adelyne" emanated from the restaurant. In August of 1943, Danny and Adelyne married.

Not only was Danny now a husband, he also became an instant father. Adelyne had a five-year old son from a previous short-lived marriage, but Danny soon developed a bond with Eddie.

In 1948, Danny and Adelyne had their first child, a boy, whom they named after Danny's brother Jack. In 1950, their second son was born and was named after Danny.

In November, 1951, Danny's mother Eva passed away at the age of eighty-five, and seven months later his father Nathan died at the age of eighty-eight. His brother Samuel died a year and a half later at the age of sixty-two followed three months later by the death of his brother David at the age of fifty-nine. In less than three years, he had lost the bulk of his family. Only his three sisters remained.

By early 1954, the Club Continental was simply not doing well enough to keep open, and Danny closed up shop. His wife Adelyne had not performed in the club for several years, as she was busy at home raising three children. The business had been tapering off ever since. Soon the family left San Francisco and moved to Los Angeles.

Adelyne and Danny Joseph in 1946

In Los Angeles, Danny worked in the casinos in Gardena acting as a greeter and on occasion "helping" with some of the casinos less reputable bookmaking activities. Danny's love of boxing, however, never waned and now that he was back in Los Angeles, the scene of his later boxing career, he would attend the occasional fight at the Olympic Auditorium.

It was while he was attending a match at the Olympic that he had occasion to run into a fellow former boxer from the old days. That fighter's name was Mickey Cohen. Mickey Cohen never made a name for himself boxing in the ring, but later became a notorious Los Angeles mobster. Cohen had worked for Al Capone in Chicago after his boxing days were over but eventually moved to Los Angeles to work for another Jewish mobster, Bugsy Siegel. After Siegel died, Cohen took the top spot in Los Angeles.

Danny and Cohen spoke about old times while at the Olympic Auditorium and Cohen invited Danny to come over to his house for a card game later that week. Danny accepted the invitation and showed up at Cohen's house for a friendly card game. Only this game didn't end well. Shortly after the game began, it was raided by the police. Cohen and Danny weren't close friends, so Cohen immediately felt that Danny was responsible for the police raid. The two never spoke again.

Financial struggles eventually began to have their effect on Danny's marriage, so in 1957, the two separated. Danny began to drive a cab for a living after the separation and the job at the casino dried up.

Danny was devastated by the breakup because his love for Adelyne never ceased. However, their age difference, over eighteen years, and money problems eventually led to a divorce in 1959.

Danny never recovered from the breakup of his marriage, however he was a devoted father who stayed close to his children. But as the years progressed Danny also began suffering from the lasting effects of his boxing career. His memory was beginning to lapse and he was starting to show signs of paranoia. While he could recount his boxing career in detail, he had difficulty remembering the smaller details of everyday life.

This didn't stop him from attempting marriage one more time, marrying again in early 1963. However, that marriage, too, only lasted a short while and Danny was single again by 1964.

By 1966, with the effects of his boxing career taking its toll, he could no longer manage his own affairs and his sister Edith became his guardian. When he could no longer drive he gave his car to his son, Danny. Danny lived a meager life, but his paranoia led to his belief that his sister was stealing money from him. Consequently, Edith eventually relinquished her guardianship of Danny to a public guardian.

In November of 1967 Danny received a call from his son, Danny informing him that Adelyne had died suddenly of a heart attack at the age of forty-six. Danny cried like a baby. On the day of the funeral, Danny had difficulty composing himself.

Just three months later, on the morning of February 28, 1968, Danny started his day as he always had since he began boxing nearly a half century ago. He began his regimen of calisthenics but began to feel ill. He sat down at the foot of his bed, suffered a massive heart attack, and died at the age of sixty-four. When he died, he lived in an apartment at 236 Sycamore in Los Angeles, just down the street from where his brother Jack had died.

When Moishe Josofsky came to the United States in 1911, he was a Russian Jewish immigrant with little more than he was able to carry. While many other Jewish immigrants were struggling to make a living, Moishe had carved a niche for himself as a professional prizefighter named Dandy Dillon becoming a boxing champion. He left this earth with little more than what he brought from Russia, but he left a legacy for his children, grandchildren, and great grandchildren that will endure the test of time.

Danny with Sons Jack and Danny (the author) in 1963

AUTHOR'S NOTE

Writing the story of my father's life was a labor of love. I was fortunate that my father kept a detailed scrapbook of most of his boxing matches. That, along with the Internet and the ability to search newspaper archives made this task much easier. I have attempted to detail his boxing career with as much accuracy as I possibly could and am happy with the results. I was only seventeen when I lost my father but have never stopped thinking about him. I wrote this book as a lasting tribute to him.

I would also like to thank my wife, Ivy, who was invaluable in the editing of this book. Given that this book was self-published, I relied heavily on her help.

DANDY DILLON'S BOXING RECORD

#	DATE	OPPONENT	LOCATION	DEC	RND	Cumul. Record
1	3-Jan-1920	Frankie Gilman	Minneapolis, Minnesota	W	4	1-0-0
2	1-Feb-1920	Jimmy Valentine	Eveleth, Minnesota	W	6	2-0-0
3	6-May-1920	Percy Buzza	Fort Francis, Ontario, Canada	W	10	3-0-0
4	25-Jun-1920	Al Norton	Nicolette Park, Minnesota	W	4	4-0-0
5	11-Aug-1920	Young Mendo	Buffalo, New York	W	10	5-0-0
6	14-Aug-1920	Benny Vogel	Rochester, Minnesota	ND	10	5-0-1
7	3-Sep-1920	Johnny Ecklund	Nicollet Park, Minnesota	W KO	2	6-0-1
8	6-Sep-1920	Battling Baker	Duluth, Minnesota	W KO	2	7-0-1
9	17-Sep-1920	Jimmy Kelly	La Suer, Minnesota	W KO	3	8-0-1
10	10-Oct-1920	Benny Vogel	Mankato, Minnesota	ND	10	8-0-2
11	1-Nov-1920	Kewpie Callender	Minneapolis, Minnesota	ND	10	8-0-3
12	12-Nov-1920	Stewart McLean	Minneapolis, Minnesota	ND	10	8-0-4
13	8-Dec-1920	Percy Buzza	Winnepeg, Canada	W KO	9	9-0-4
14	21-Jan-1921	Jimmy Valentine	Duluth, Minnesota	W	6	10-0-4
15	22-Feb-1921	Frankie Mason	Des Moines, Iowa	L	10	10-1-4
16	14-Mar-1921	Eddie White	Detroit, Michigan	W	10	11-1-4
17	29-Apr-1921	Frankie Jumatti	Cedar Rapids, Iowa	W	10	12-1-4
18	6-May-1921	Frankie Mason	Cedar Rapids, Iowa	W	10	13-1-4
19	4-Jul-1921	Ray Rose	Butte, Montana	ND	15	13-1-5
20	1-Nov-1921	Benny Mertens	Rochester, Minnesota	W	10	14-1-5
21	23-Jan-1922	Jimmy Tomasuto	Newark, New Jersey	W	8	15-1-5
22	18-Aug-1922	Eddie Nemo	Hibbing, Minnesota	W KO	9	16-1-5
23	4-Sep-1922	Cyclone Yeisky	Omaha, Nebraska	W KO	1	17-1-5
24	9-Oct-1922	Joey Schwartz	St. Paul, Minnesota	W	10	18-1-5
25	27-Oct-1922	Joe Burger	Denver, Colorado	L	12	18-2-5
26	29-Dec-1922	Sammy Gordon	Great Falls, Montana	W KO	12	19-2-5
27	8-Jan-1923	Lackey Morrow	Great Falls, Montana	W	12	20-2-5
28	16-Jan-1923	Young Farrell	Vernon, California	ND	4	20-2-6
29	23-Jan-1923	Tod Morgan	Vernon, California	L	4	20-3-6
30	20-Feb-1923	Johnny Lotsey	Vernon, California	L	4	20-4-6
31	6-Mar-1923	Vic Foley	Seattle, Washington	L	6	20-5-6
32	13-Mar-1923	Georgie Lee	Seattle, Washington	W	6	21-5-6
33	20-Mar-1923	Vic Foley	Seattle, Washington	W	12	22-5-6
34	17-Apr-1923	Mike DePinto	Butte, Montana	W	12	23-5-6
35	1-May-1923	California Joe Lynch	Seattle, Washington	ND	12	23-5-7
36	2-Sep-1923	Weldon "Tuffy" Wing	Butte, Montana	W	12	24-5-7
37	12-Sep-1923	Tod Morgan	Seattle, Washington	ND	6	24-5-8
38	26-Sep-1923	Tod Morgan	Seattle, Washington	L DQ	4	24-6-8
39	2-Nov-1923	Frankie Brown	Hollywood, California	W	4	25-6-8
40	7-Dec-1923	Joe Bell	Stockton, California	W KO	2	26-6-8
41	14-Dec-1923	Dynamite Joe Murphy	Stockton, California	W	4	27-6-8
42	1-Jan-1924	Joe King Leopold	Oakland, California	L	4	27-7-8
43	11-Jan-1924	Frankie Garcia	Hollywood, California	L	4	27-8-8
44	5-Feb-1924	Larry Murphy	Vernon, California	ND	4	27-8-9
45	22-Feb-1924	Eddie Anderson	Hollywood, California	L	4	27-9-9
46	4-Mar-1924	Larry Murphy	Vernon, California	ND	4	27-9-10
47	25-Apr-1924	Len Malody	Vancouver, Canada	L	10	27-10-10
48	1-May-1924	Bud Ridley	Tacoma, Washington	L	4	27-11-10
49	11-Aug-1924	Ray Miller	Aurora, Illinois	L KO	6	27-12-10
50	8-Oct-1924	Billy Hogan	Wilmington, California	W	4	28-12-10
51	22-Oct-1924	Benny Dotson	Wilmington, California	ND	4	28-12-11
52	5-Nov-1924	Benny Dotson	Wilmington, California	ND	4	28-12-12
53	19-Nov-1924	Ritchie King	Wilmington, California	ND	4	28-12-13
54	6-Feb-1925	Gene Delmont	Hollywood, California	L	6	28-13-13
55	11-Feb-1925	Pico Ramies	Wilmington, California	W	8	29-13-13
56	25-Feb-1925	Ritchie King	Wilmington, California	L	10	29-14-13
57	16-Sep-1925	Frankie Garcia	Los Angeles, California	L	6	29-15-13
58	13-Oct-1925	Kid Kopecks	Fresno, California	L KO	10	29-16-13
59	6-Apr-1926	Len Malody	Portland, Oregon	L	1	29-17-13
60	4-May-1927	Tony Cruz	El Rio, California	W	8	30-17-13
61	25-May-1927	Pico Ramies	Wilmington, California	L TKO	6	30-18-13

WINS	30
KNOCKOUTS	8
LOSES	18
NO DECISIONS	13
TOTAL FIGHTS	61
TOTAL ROUNDS	423

11782995R0009

Made in the USA
Lexington, KY
31 October 2011